Root Cellar

The Ultimate Guide to Building a Root Cellar

(A Comprehensive Beginner's Guide to Learn the Best Methods to Build)

Joshua Thompson

Published By **Bella Frost**

Joshua Thompson

All Rights Reserved

Root Cellar: The Ultimate Guide to Building a Root Cellar (A Comprehensive Beginner's Guide to Learn the Best Methods to Build)

ISBN 978-0-9938301-9-8

No part of this guidebook shall be reproduced in any form without permission in writing from the publisher except in the case of brief quotations embodied in critical articles or reviews.

Legal & Disclaimer

The information contained in this book is not designed to replace or take the place of any form of medicine or professional medical advice. The information in this book has been provided for educational & entertainment purposes only.

The information contained in this book has been compiled from sources deemed reliable, and it is accurate to the best of the Author's knowledge; however, the Author cannot guarantee its accuracy and validity and cannot be held liable for any errors or omissions. Changes are periodically made to this book. You must consult your doctor or get professional medical advice before using any of the suggested remedies, techniques, or information in this book.

Upon using the information contained in this book, you agree to hold harmless the Author from and against any damages, costs, and expenses, including any legal fees potentially resulting from the application of any of the information provided by this guide. This disclaimer applies to any damages or injury caused by the use and application, whether directly or indirectly, of any advice or information presented, whether for breach of contract, tort, negligence, personal injury, criminal intent, or under any other cause of action.

You agree to accept all risks of using the information presented inside this book. You need to consult a professional medical practitioner in order to ensure you are both able and healthy enough to participate in this program.

Table Of Contents

Chapter 1: What Is Root Cellaring? 1

Chapter 2: Basics of Root Cellaring 22

Chapter 3: Root Cellar Designs 44

Chapter 4: Root Cellar Organization Tips 68

Chapter 5: What to Store in a Root Cellar 89

Chapter 6: Harvesting and Preparing ... 113

Chapter 7: Creating Your Own Root Cellar 136

Chapter 8: Canning 165

Chapter 1: What Is Root Cellaring?

Before the supply of power and domestic equipment like refrigerators, root cellars were used to save sparkling produce, stopping the meals from freezing in wintry weather and keeping it cool at some point of warmness summer time days. For some a long time, root cellars appeared obsolete because of facilities like modern-day refrigeration. However, extended pursuits in sustainable residing, gardening, and food safety have revived the usage of root cellars.

Root cellaring is an historical exercising that has been spherical for hundreds of years. It's a way of preserving culmination and greens by using way of storing them in a groovy, darkish region. An underground chamber or a room interior your own home is created to be used as a root cellar. Root cellaring lets in you to save produce at a regular temperature, amongst 32 and forty tiers Fahrenheit, and high humidity ranging amongst 80-ninety%. These conditions keep your culmination and greens clean for months at a time. In this bankruptcy, we'll undergo root cellars, their motive, their records, and the benefits of the use of one.

What Is a Root Cellar?

Root cellars are systems buried partly or completely inside the floor and are clearly used to preserve root vegetation, cease stop result, vegetables, and other food types as a manner to rot or might spoil if neglected within the open. These systems can preserve meals for months, relying at the form of crop and the climate conditions.

The soil, or earth as we understand it, is a awful conductor of warmth. This soil function allows root cellars to keep a normal inner temperature. A few feet beneath the ground, the temperature remains cool and everyday, no matter the out of doors weather conditions. This balance makes root cellars art work like natural refrigeration gadgets. The moisture inside the soil affords to the effectiveness of keeping meals, as excessive humidity degrees are a essential problem of storing substances.

The dust beneath the foundation cellar maintains a everyday temperature that prolongs the storage duration of the meals devices. At the identical time, the excessive humidity prevents produce from drying out. The temperature inside the cellar is critical and need to be stored amongst 32 and forty five ranges Fahrenheit. The best variety for relative humidity is among eighty% and 90%.

Specifically, it prevents the growth of microorganisms that could destroy natural foods and slows the ethylene gas produced by means of the saved meals gadgets. Humidity stages prevent water from evaporating out of the air. Vegetables maintain maximum of their dietary charge and taste profile even after being saved for a long time. However, numerous food devices like clean meat are not appropriate.

The History of Root Cellars

Those born after the big availability of refrigerators may not recognize the massive role root cellars performed within the agricultural enterprise. For a millennial or a Gen-Z kid, a root cellar have to appear like now not some thing extra than a jumble of stones propped up toward a hillside. Traditional root cellars had been product of stone, on the equal time because the floor end up included with clay. Their today's duration at the time have become 20*20*10 ft in duration.

Every unmarried home at a few stage within the 17th and 18th centuries had a root cellar crafted from easily to be had substances. To keep meals from spoiling, a root cellar uses the soil's insulating competencies to hold the temperature above freezing inside the wintry climate and below freezing in the summer time. The form keeps clearly the right temperature and humidity to prevent bacterial boom and allow the meals gadgets to stay glowing for longer intervals. Vegetables harvested within the fall had been stored in the root cellar, which protected potatoes, turnips, and carrots. In evaluation, meals gadgets like beets, onions, preserves/jams, salt pork, salt, and salt fish were stored inside the root cellar for the wintry weather. Farmers dwelling in enormously cold environments furthermore fed their animals with food stores of their cellars.

In the nineteenth century, root cellars started out for use to maintain harvests until the middle of wintry weather and allowed the ones food gadgets to be offered for a higher rate. During the struggle, root cellars moreover served as safehouses for fleeing prisoners and enslaved people.

Other uses of root cellars at the time covered their use as software program software rooms or possibly laundry facilities. Root cellars have been significantly utilized to maintain animal feed, but the amount had to get the animals via the wintry weather may require a far large storage facility than the same old period.

People had been endorsed to shop food and use their root cellars, inside the event that they'd them, or to have new ones constructed by using manner of the use of the Office of War Information and the Farm Security Administration throughout the Great Depression and World War II. Everyone end up suggested to keep resources via extending the shelf lifestyles of perishable gadgets. This proposal have emerge as little by little popular some of the farmers as extra people began witnessing the maintaining consequences the form furnished. Selecting a likely location and figuring out soil with the right quantity of moisture emerge as sensitive through the years.

Your superb bet for a root cellar is to dig at least four toes down and discover a spot where the temperature remains beneath forty five ranges Fahrenheit at some stage in the year. Over time, people started out storing garlic paper, hooks, dried beans, potatoes in piles (now and again buried in the sand), apples in bushels, and cured meat hung from hooks, frequently blanketed in a fabric bag.

Most households in advance than and after World War II had fewer financial belongings and couldn't manipulate to pay for a fridge. Therefore, maximum people relied on this much less pricey technique of storing food objects for longer intervals, permitting them to consume food inside the path of the year or even promote their flora for a higher income. It's now not possibly that the idea cellar will reappear so long as we've were given freezers, but it became essential to the survival of many Americans for generations.

Why Root Cellars Are Becoming Popular Again

Installing a root cellar offers homesteaders an multiplied feeling of independence because it's an inexperienced and sustainable shape constituted of pretty honestly available herbal substances. Due to the large availability of fridges, rapid urbanization, and technological upgrades, root cellars are not crucial for the normal individual. However, homesteaders can take into account retaining off dependence on the grid via building a cellar underneath floor. If you have got one, you obtained't need to worry approximately perishables going terrible inside the occasion of a strength outage.

Environmentally-Friendly

Although modern refrigerators, particularly those with Energy Star certification, are appreciably extra electricity-green than previous fashions, they nonetheless account for a disproportionately large percent of widespread strength use. Worldwide, nearly two hundred million fridges are offered yearly, and in the United States on my own, ninety nine.8 percentage of all households have and make normal use of a fridge. There are about 129 million families within the United States, and a present day refrigerator makes use of approximately four hundred-kilowatt hours (kWh) of energy yearly on commonplace. This manner that fridges in the United States use more than 50 billion kWh of strength each 12 months, contributing to risky emissions and growing the carbon footprint. If you need to hold cash in your power bill and lessen your impact at the environment, reducing again in your family's power consumption need to be a essential goal. If you have room for a root cellar, you may use this sensible food garage option and remove the second one fridge altogether.

Carbon Footprint

The international food machine in recent times involves the use of chemical substances, heavy machinery, plastics, and additional inside the growing, harvesting, and packaging of food gadgets. Purchasing forestall quit end result and veggies are grown on an business degree although produces numerous via-merchandise which might be harmful to the surroundings. Recently, the fashion of developing natural meals the usage of sustainable, harvesting, and storing them the usage of green strategies are gaining reputation.

In the vain of wintry weather, glowing fruit and greens from the grocery store have surely traveled loads of miles to reap your desk. According to the Center for Urban Education on Sustainable Agriculture, the average American meal travels spherical 1,500 miles from its farm of origin on your table, contributing to a big boom in greenhouse gas emissions. Apples from Chile or soybeans from Argentina to your property in New York will make contributions notably to the ones risky gas emissions. With the help of a root cellar, your circle of relatives need to have yr-round access to sustainable, nearby, and occasional-emission food on the same time as showing their manual for nearby farmers and agricultural industries. However, this may most effective be finished whilst sustainable farming practices and associated techniques are used.

Limiting Chemicals

When it includes fitness, it's crucial to phrase that the globalized food tool necessitates using severa chemical materials to maintain meals in the path of its extended adventure spherical the arena. These are a number of the most usually used compounds for extending the shelf existence of forestall stop end result, vegetables, and particular meals: The effective fungicide sodium ortho-phenyl phenate (SOPP) prevents the increase of mold and fungi on meals merchandise. Thiabendazole is an effective fungicide used on numerous prevent result and veggies.

Likewise, maleic hydrazide prevents citrus end result from budding and reasons them to head dormant. Many European global places have banned those poisonous chemical substances. After harvest, the crops are also sprayed with sulfuryl fluoride, an insecticide, to boom their viability and storage life. However, this spray deposits substantial tiers of fluoride on meals, which leads a few households to strive to influence smooth of it. The fitness dangers associated with the modern food supply chain are severa. Still, they can be appreciably mitigated with the aid of adopting inexperienced farming techniques and using sustainable techniques to keep organically produced factors like a root cellar.

The best performance of a root cellar is predicated upon on keeping a selected temperature and humidity stage. Aside from that, a root cellar is similar to an underground bunker or garage area. This way that you may use your creativeness to expand various specific root cellar plans, protective the whole thing from the most honest designs to the most complicated ones. Several materials, which incorporates timber, cement, stone, clay, and similar manufacturing substances, may be used as long as the required temperature and humidity live on the preferred degrees.

The most clean design of a root cellar is a plant storage area made from a barrel. Fruits and greens may be saved in a barrel or buried in the floor. This technique works further to some other root cellaring design and is one of the most inexpensive ones. However, those make-shift root cellars can not replace traditional bunker-like root cellars. A desired root cellar is a tremendous underground room where plants can stay preserved with out the danger of pests. It has an outdoor door, retaining its the front ruin unfastened the principle house. While some decide upon building those root cellars adjoining to the house, others assemble them close to their crop fields or assemble a cave-like room in hilly terrain to feature a root cellar. Putting a root cellar on a hill has the introduced advantage of simplifying excavation.

Initially, the famous root cellar format have become an underground structure dug into the floor, developing a garage area. A domestic or a shed modified into ideally built on the ones root cellars, permitting better get proper of entry to to the saved items with out going far in the crop fields or areas a ways from domestic. Concealed passageways like a entice door within the shed or a hatch from the storage were associated with the foundation cellar in case the out of doors door have grow to be blocked because of heavy snow or comparable climate situations.

With time, root cellars advanced. Another famous way come to be to gather a root cellar much like a room via way of the use of stacking rocks to create the partitions and reinforcing them with clay. This approach changed into thru and massive applied in regions in which digging underground changed into not possible and could have an impact on the encompassing terrain.

Benefits of a Root Cellar

There are severa advantages to root-cellaring your produce. For starters, having food saved away for the wintry climate, making sure you'll have an ok supply of food, is constantly a deliver of consolation. Even if the meals supply chain halts for a few motive, you'll be self-sufficient. The food stored in a root cellar can be loved all wintry climate with out dropping electricity on transportation. The flowers, greens, and culmination you beautify or benefit domestically at the peak of harvest are extra fee-powerful than those bought in some unspecified time within the destiny of wintry climate from the grocery shop. Proper root-cellaring might also even take away the requirement for a freezer or canning your meals while completed the proper way.

There are greater health benefits to ingesting seasonal food. Beta-carotene, antioxidants, and phytochemicals decided in squashes, carrots, and one-of-a-kind roots supply our bodies a further line of protection in opposition to the common cold in the fall and wintry weather, and the complex carbohydrates in those veggies hold us energized despite the fact that the times are brief and the temperature drops.

Unfortunately, because of improvements inside the home advent organisation, root-cellaring has emerge as one of the least powerful traditional strategies of keeping meals. The conventional root cellar had a clay floor and stone or brick partitions to maintain the contents cool and wet. Without model, the finished basements and urban floors of current-day houses with primary heating systems do now not provide the best conditions for prolonged-term storage of produce. Nonetheless, nearly any vicinity can be modified for root-cellaring with enough have a observe and knowledge approximately the development, keeping the right temperatures, and using suitable substances to meet the necessities.

Here are a few exclusive blessings of root cellaring:

A root cellar is a shape that imitates and works with nature.

It can artwork effectively with out grid energy and doesn't require electricity like a refrigerator.

Unlike a fridge or a few one of a kind garage tool, there are not any transferring additives that could malfunction.

Constructing a root cellar allows you to spend a whole lot plenty much less cash on payments.

The operation costs are essentially zero, due to the fact the essential substances used for building a root cellar can be without trouble salvaged.

Having a root cellar lets in you to shop for items in large portions at extensively lower expenses, storing them for low season use.

It can be pointless to have a freezer or a 2d fridge, mainly for food devices, if you understand the way to apply the root cellar.

Risks like immoderate weather, pandemics, geopolitical tensions, and financial instability can disrupt food deliver chains. Having a root cellar guarantees you've got adequate meals in your own family with out counting on food supply chains.

Using sustainable garage strategies, like a root cellar, is an inexperienced contribution. Using these strategies can beneficial resource in protective the Earth and doing all your thing in reducing volatile fuel emissions.

While a root cellar doesn't at once lessen the carbon dioxide emissions inside the air, the regenerative agriculture practices applied in developing flora sustainably are one of the key methods to restriction the amount of carbon dioxide inside the environment.

You received't be contributing in the path of waste from product packaging as your meals can be locally sourced produce.

It shortens the time span food takes to tour to our tables and promotes the increase of nearby manufacturers.

Root cellaring lets in hold cash inner our network's monetary device

Fruits and veggies need to best be root-cellared if they will be sparkling and healthy. When storing meals in the root cellar, look for any holes, nicks, bruises, bugs, or distinct signs and symptoms and signs and symptoms and signs of harm to the food. Always take the time inspecting meals, in particular at the same time as making ready for winter garage. Storing low-great food having one or a couple of symptoms of meals harm will best motive the boom of microorganisms at the manner to finally rot the meals. Damaged food can be consumed quickly or preserved in a jar or freezer bag. For instance, apples and pears can be become sauce, squash may be roasted and frozen, and beets may be pickled.

Make ordinary journeys to the muse cellar to check out the stored food often. Even if one awful fruit or vegetable goes terrible and stays ignored for some days, it could damage each one-of-a-kind saved object. It's vital to dispose of any spoiled gadgets right away and take a look at for signs and symptoms of pests or mildew. Additionally, pay attention to the temperature and humidity levels, and modify them as wanted. It's additionally an amazing concept to rotate the stored gadgets in order that the older ones are used in advance than they have got a chance to break. Regularly analyzing your root cellar will ensure that the saved meals stays sparkling and secure to consume.

It's vital to put in some leg paintings. You'll want to take a look at and take a look at in advance than getting the most from your root cellar. For example, you'll want to discover ways to maintain the inspiration cellar ground damp, take away mould and mildew from growing, often dispose of spoiled meals during the inspection, and manage the spread of pests. The manufacturing of a root cellar is a time-eating and pricey task that might take severa weeks or maybe months, depending on the terrific of the substances you pick and the layout you need for the muse cellar.

Besides retaining produce, root cellaring saves you cash by way of using allowing you to shop for in bulk and take advantage of seasonal earnings. It's an smooth and within your manner manner to make certain that your meals is as smooth and nutritious as viable. If you're trying to hold your produce and hold money, root cellaring is genuinely some thing you want to keep in thoughts!

Chapter 2: Basics of Root Cellaring

A root cellar have to meet three minimal necessities. The greater you observe those three topics, the longer your produce will remaining. High humidity in a root cellar is essential for storing meals objects successfully. Humidity ranges among ninety% and ninety five% are exceptional for storing most root greens and vegetables. Keeping the environment moist and humid is a primary manner of preserving culmination and greens while keeping the garage location free from microorganisms and pests.

Your primary hassle need to be the temperature inside the root cellar. When nicely constructed, a root cellar continues its frigid temperature with the resource of the use of borrowing bloodless. You can "borrow" bloodless thru digging underneath floor, wherein the temperature is a consistent fifty tiers Fahrenheit. By starting a window or a closable exhaust pipe at night time time, cold air from out of doors can be borrowed and used to preserve the cellar on the right temperature.

Try to constantly preserve the temperature among 32 and forty ranges Fahrenheit. Root veggies and apples may be stored for shorter intervals in a temperature shape of forty to 50 ranges, while onions and special short-lived flowers like peppers, tomatoes, and eggplant may be saved for a most of a month or .

The section close to the roof of an indoor root cellar may be a few levels hotter than the region near the floor; this mild temperature distinction may be used to hold greens consistent with their precise wishes.

A root cellar can't characteristic well without a thermometer. You can mark the thermometer for the minimal and maximum temperatures to make it much less complicated to adjust air float.

Humidity Levels

A root cellar's humidity degree have to be stored high to hold the vegetables from drying out and dropping flavor and vitamins. High-water-content material fabric vegetables like potatoes, carrots, and beets start to dry in low-humidity environments. As a give up stop result, they are capable of dry up and lose their taste. However, different cease give up result and greens can decay or extend mold if the humidity is clearly too immoderate. Most root vegetables thrive in a wet environment from ninety five% to 98%. A humidifier or a basin of water saved in the root cellar can preserve a everyday humidity degree. The freshness and shelf existence of stored vegetables may be superior with the aid of manner of manner of controlling the humidity in a root cellar.

There are 3 installed strategies to hold the humidity ranges in a root cellar. It's first-rate initially a dirt floor because it will take in and maintain more moisture than a difficult floor like concrete or stone walls. To keep the floor's moisture, scatter gravel on pinnacle of compacted earth, preserving the moisture locked in and preventing the unfold of dust to specific areas of the foundation cellar. However, the humidity within the storage area drops below a positive threshold. In that case, you need to feature extra moisture with the useful resource of sprinkling water at the gravel, on the way to in the long run seep into the floor.

The 2nd method to maintain humidity is thru sprinkling water on the ground, laying damp however now not dripping moist burlap luggage on top of the saved food gadgets, or placing some pans of water at the ground of the foundation cellar. Keeping the moisture degree excessive is critical within the autumn at the same time as food garage starts offevolved offevolved offevolved. Root veggies may be stored with out issues in clean bins. These greens can preserve their silky and enterprise texture even in humid areas. However, a 3rd method can also show greater effective if the humidity levels fall too low in spite of attempting the number one strategies. You can use wet sawdust, sand, or moss to % the vegetables, especially carrots, beets, and parsnips, reducing the amount of moisture misplaced via the leaves.

Cooler air extensively decreases the humidity levels than warmer air. A volatile surroundings is created even as excessive cold and excessive humidity comes throughout every specific. The air becomes in reality saturated with moisture on the equal time because the temperature drops from 34 to 32 levels Fahrenheit. At that component, the temperature is called the dew factor, wherein water vapors in the air begin condensing on cold surfaces like walls, ceilings, or even greens. The stored produce is extra susceptible to spoiling if it turns into damp, even at cool temperatures. A hygrometer offers you the best humidity degrees, which makes it an awful lot much less complicated to regulate therefore.

Lighting Conditions

Root cellars are underground garage rooms dug into the floor or built right right right into a hillside to offer the same cool, dark environment as underground caves. The low temperature and darkness are important at the same time as retaining the meals glowing for extended intervals.

Root cellar end end result and vegetables are vulnerable to premature ripening and spoilage if exposed to mild. This is why most root cellars are constructed to have little or no (if any) natural mild. If artificial lighting is used, low-wattage bulbs are normally used, and the bulbs are normally covered to reduce the quantity of moderate achieving the fruit.

Ventilation

The layout of a root cellar's air waft gadget is crucial to maintaining the temperature and humidity degrees maximum suitable for preserving fruits and vegetables. Natural air go with the waft structures in root cellars use the stack impact of airflow to maintain a consistent temperature and humidity.

The air in a root cellar with herbal air flow enters via openings in the ground. These openings allow in cool, dry air from outdoor, preserving the fine temperature and humidity for preserving the produce easy. Vents or air shops on the pinnacle of the form launch the first-class and at ease, humid air from the foundation cellar. This continues the premise cellar from becoming a breeding ground for mildew and mold, which may also in any other case break the produce stored there. Root veggies and fruits can generate risky gases like carbon dioxide (CO_2) and ethylene. Therefore, it's essential to hold the basis cellar ventilated to keep them from building up. Produce may be stored glowing and free of risky molds with the help of a well constructed ventilation system.

It's critical to tweak the air float every time the climate adjustments. For instance, much less airflow is needed to save you the indoors from being overly dry within the warmer months. In assessment, more airflow is crucial for the chillier months to hold the indoors from becoming excessively wet and humid.

In a nutshell, the relationship among root cellars and air flow is that the latter is vital for retaining the premise cellar at the fine temperature, humidity, and airflow. Those subjects maintain the freshness and growth the shelf lifestyles of the fruit saved inner.

Bringing sparkling air right right into a root cellar, controlling the airflow, and making sure that it circulates are the basics of right air flow. Keeping the distance ventilated keeps the perfect temperature required to keep produce. Likewise, controlling the airflow can lessen stifling humidity and condensation because of a temperature alternate.

The warm air inside the root cellar will rise whilst the cold air travels close to the ground. If you want to get the most out of the air waft to your place, vicinity the intake low and the hollow excessive, preferably on considered one in all a type walls. The low intake will permit cool air in, whilst the hole will set free the fine and comfy air. It can be enough to put in a single, excessive-placed exhaust vent in a small storage space thru which air can enter. Remember to raise the crates a few inches above the floor to allow air to go with the flow under, preventing the meals devices from getting stale.

Other Factors to Consider When Building a Root Cellar

A root cellar will handiest thrive if it's far inside the proper area; except finding an opening wherein it can hold the gold trendy temperature and humidity, it is crucial to test the soil and the opportunity of water harm.

You need to appearance some area else if there is a immoderate water diploma or a close-by flow into or river.

Insulation

Putting insulation in the root cellar can preserve the temperature strong and save you warmth from escaping. Root cellars can be insulated the usage of fiberglass, cellulose, foam, or some unique insulation fabric used inside the manufacturing company. Besides reducing the power needed to keep an appropriate temperature within the root cellar, insulation also can help in preventing moisture from escaping. The root cellar's walls, ground, and ceiling want to be insulated.

A extremely good root cellar can also have abilties that allow you to modify the temperature and humidity to keep your end result and greens smooth for extended intervals. Vents or air inlets installed at the bottom of the shape and vents or air outputs set up at the pinnacle are current strategies for accomplishing this aim. By permitting cool, dry air from outside and freeing warm temperature, wet air, these vents help in preserving the foundation cellar's indoors at perfect stages for storing fruit. If you want to recognize whilst to open or near the vents, a thermometer/hygrometer let you.

Water Damage

If your root cellar is experiencing water damage due to heavy rainfall, the inner temperature and humidity tiers will become tough to preserve. This water damage or flooding within the root cellar may be results prevented if proper drainage is installed. A sump pump and drainage machine is probably constructed at the same time as there's too much water. This is important to keep the basis cellar and its contents in appropriate condition.

Additionally, it's crucial to make sure that the premise cellar's basis is constructed above the water desk and product of water-evidence materials, together with concrete. The walls and ground of the idea cellar need to furthermore be made of impervious substances or blanketed with a water-resistant membrane if it is constructed underground. A drainage system also may be hooked up throughout the outer edge of the premise cellar to divert water a ways from the muse. This may be done with the useful resource of digging a trench around the root cellar's exterior and filling it with gravel.

Another vital element to go through in mind is proper air waft. Vents or air inlets should be established at the bottom of the foundation cellar to deliver inside the easy air, and ducts or air shops need to be set up at the pinnacle to launch stale air. This will assist to regulate the moisture stage in the root cellar, as a end end result reducing the hazard of mildew boom. It's important to keep up with normal renovation and inspections of the basis cellar to come to be privy to capability troubles earlier than they enhance.

Insect and Rat Control

A well-sealed root cellar with few get admission to elements can keep unwanted pests from wreaking havoc in your harvest. Sealant or caulking ought to be used to fill in any and all openings. Also, cleanliness and the removal of discarded meals need to be priorities.

It's vital to use hermetic packing containers for storing produce. Mason jars or one-of-a-kind glass containers are first-rate for this cause as they keep insects out and hold the taste of the produce for an extended term. Insect traps also are a extremely good way to govern insect populations to your root cellar or specific meals garage location. Place bait inside the entice – this could encompass quantities of fruit or greens – and vicinity them in strategic locations throughout your garage area. The insects may be attracted with the useful resource of the use of the scent of meals, get trapped inner, and sooner or later die because of lack of oxygen. Natural insect repellents together with diatomaceous earth also can be used to maintain bugs faraway from stored produce. Sprinkle a thin layer of the powder at some stage in the storage vicinity, ensuring to cover all cracks and crevices which can offer get right of access to elements for insects. Reapply after sweeping or vacuuming. With the ones precautions in region, you may protect your saved produce from pests and make certain it stays sparkling for so long as possible.

The root cellar wishes to be with out hassle available for cleansing and harvesting. It's most convenient if it's near the kitchen and needs a sturdy, lockable door.

Think approximately how a good deal meals you'll save inside the root cellar, then assemble it therefore. The root cellar want to be massive sufficient to hold all of the meals you have to hold however no longer so large that air can't circulate. If you need extra room for storage than you currently have, maintain in mind adding some degrees or shelves. Remember that all of these factors are interconnected and that clever desire-making in a unmarried region might also additionally have knock-on results on others. If you need to ensure your root cellar is constructed to final and fits your desires, it's outstanding to consult a expert builder.

Tweaking Your Root Cellar

The shape of root cellar you deliver collectively or alter can be determined by means of things collectively with your property's format, the topography of your land, and the not unusual annual temperature and quantity of snowstorm to your location.

You're fortunate if your own home has a basement with a dirt floor. You can short flip the gap into an first rate meals storage cellar with some adjustments. Even in a domestic with a heated basement, an unheated section can be sectioned off and used for storing greens.

Dig right right into a hillside for an out of doors root cellar, or pass underground and cover the access with a bulkhead door, patio, or porch. The most common locations for outdoor root cellars are within the earth at the north (and because of this coldest) problem of the residence or dug right proper into a north-going thru hill. Some of the older, underground root cellars face south, making them extra to be had inside the winter.

Climbing into an under-porch garage hollow may be more appealing than digging via snow drifts to reach a hill-cave root cellar in case you stay in which wintry climate temperatures frequently drop below zero levels Fahrenheit. Like the only examined below, many underground root cellars have an anteroom or double doors that shape an airlock to keep heat summer season air out of the cellar and save you immoderate fruit cooling in the extreme wintry weather cold.

You will most effective be capable of get your cellar all of the way down to the exceptional temperature for storing root greens in case your winters are slight, with not unusual temperatures a long way over 30 levels

Fahrenheit. The garden row need to be high-quality for those veggies, and an exceptional vicinity of the residence have to do the trick for the top notch and snug-keepers like squash, onions, and candy potatoes.

People decide upon areas as a minimum eight feet with the aid of manner of 10 ft in length, although they not often advantage capacity (a 5-with the aid of-8-foot place can preserve 30 bushels of produce). An region of 8 feet through the usage of 8 ft may be top sufficient for storing soil in buckets for greens which includes celery. Several cabinets are endorsed so that each one available areas may be utilized. Slat for air go along with the flow and handiest use rot-evidence woods. A cleat of 1 to two inches massive have to be hooked up inside the back of the cabinets to maintain the corners from touching the wall.

Fresh tomatoes, fragile dandelion shoots, almonds, pears, and cantaloupes can all be preserved with an efficiently designed root cellar.

Root cellars want to be designed with proper drainage to keep away from floods and water harm that would in any other case damage the meals saved interior. Some important elements to remember when making plans a root cellar's drainage device are as follows:

Location Decisions

Choosing a place on your root cellar that has proper drainage and isn't always scenario to flooding or excessive rains is important. Knowing the close by water desk and some exceptional belongings of water that might damage the foundation cellar is essential. The root cellar need to be constructed on slightly extended ground or on a slope which will drain water far from the building.

Additionally, it's critical to recollect the surrounding surroundings while selecting a vicinity to your root cellar. The soil type, community climate, and weather styles must all be taken into consideration. For example, if the vicinity is susceptible to high winds or heavy snow fall, the premise cellar should be built with the ones situations in mind. A robust foundation and proper insulation will assist guard the idea cellar from the ones factors.

Another crucial consideration whilst choosing a place is get proper of entry to. The root cellar need to be with out troubles available for each harvesting and cleaning. It need to be located close to the kitchen for convenience and feature a sturdy, lockable door for protection. It's additionally an amazing idea to have it in an area that is without problem accessible in case of emergencies.

In addition to the ones practical issues, it's moreover important to hold in thoughts the area's aesthetic. A root cellar can be a first rate addition to any property, however it ought to combination in with the encircling landscape and supplement the format of the house.

Ultimately, the place of your root cellar is a essential aspect of its achievement. By taking the time to carefully don't forget all the factors involved, you may ensure that your root cellar is built in an opening with a purpose to protect it and your saved produce from the elements and other capability dangers even as moreover being a handy and appealing addition to your home.

Costs of Building a Root Cellar

Building a root cellar may be a substantial funding, with prices numerous counting on factors together with length, substances, location, level of completing, and insulation degree. A number one root cellar can rate everywhere from some hundred to three thousand greenbacks, at the same time as a larger, more complex shape can with out issue reach tens of hundreds of bucks. It's important to preserve in mind that those estimates do no longer account for allows, labor, or extra charges that may be required.

When planning your root cellar, it's important to undergo in thoughts the functionality for flooding and water harm. The foundation want to be built above the water table and out of water-evidence materials, even as walls and flooring need to be built of impervious substances or coated with a water-evidence membrane. A sump pump and drainage device can also be used to take away water and divert it far from the foundation cellar.

Proper air flow is also essential for preserving the foundation cellar dry and decreasing the hazard of mould growth. Vents or air inlets should be installed at the lowest to carry within the smooth air, and ducts or air shops have to be set up on the pinnacle to release stale air. These vents need to be adjustable to alter the moisture diploma in the root cellar.

It's also crucial to recollect the floors of the idea cellar, which can advantage from a in addition layer of protection furnished with the resource of drainage matting. This matting allows water to permeate however prevents it from pooling on the ground, reducing the risk of mold and mold growth.

In summary, constructing a root cellar requires cautious making plans and interest of things including fee, water harm, and air go with the glide. It's recommended to talk with a professional or professional builder to get a more correct estimate and ensure that your root cellar is tailored for your goals and possibilities. Regular safety and inspections ought to additionally be completed to perceive capability issues and hold your root cellar in proper operating order.

Chapter 3: Root Cellar Designs

If you want to have glowing vegetation and greens at a few level inside the winter with out paying exorbitant charges, you need to start searching into root cellar designs.

As described inside the first chapter, a root cellar is any shape constructed definitely or in detail underground to keep root greens.

Root cellars were at the start designed to preserve root plants, however they have got considering that been tailor-made to shop other food devices, which encompass canned meals, end result, nuts, herbs, and pickled veggies. They can also feature shelters in times of unrest, natural failures, and distinct emergencies.

The root cellar's walking precept is based totally mostly on immoderate humidity (eighty-95%) and cool temperatures (32-45 Fahrenheit). Humidity provides simply sufficient moisture to maintain the veggies green on the equal time as the temperatures maintain the goods from freezing.

A root cellar may be hundreds of hard work, but it's far pretty easy to assemble. All it takes is considering some factors and using your deductions to decide which root cellar layout should artwork first-class for you.

This chapter will communicate one-of-a-type kinds of root cellar designs, elements to recall in advance than selecting a layout, and step-by means of-step commands for constructing your fine one.

Types of Root Cellars

Root cellars are to be had in severa sorts, however the ideal designs are drawn from the foremost varieties of root cellars listed under:

1. Basement Root Cellar

If you don't have enough region on your private home to assemble a root cellar, this basement cellar is simply what you want.

As the name implies, basement root cellars are constructed in your basement and can be finished with little or no coins. Because they may be underground, domestic basements are fine root cellars and could preserve your food sparkling so long as the right garage conditions are supplied.

2. Hole-in-the-Ground Cellar

Another excellent substitute for the basement root cellar is the hollow-in-the-floor cellar, that is proper if you have a restricted fee variety and vicinity. It entails digging a hole deep sufficient to cope with a discipline of your desire, as a way for use to preserve your greens. This cellar has the identical look as a integrated cellar and can keep a large amount of produce.

3. Container Root Cellar

You can use a transport subject as the mainframe for this root cellar layout. The field is buried after digging deep sufficient.

The container root cellar is usually recommended if you have a huge quantity of produce to keep because it provides an entire lot of garage space. It is also utilized by those who want to bring together a bunker.

four. Earthbag Root Cellar

As the decision shows, earthbag cellars are built through the usage of 'baggage of earth' - a combination of gravel, cement, and packed earth - to form the cellar's walls.

Earthbag root cellars provide most drainage, outstanding humidity manage, and temperature regulation. They also are very cheap and clean to use.

five. Septic Tank Root Cellar

This form of cellar is created by burying a present day septic tank inside the floor, preferably inside the shape of a raised earth mound. The pinnacle is then blanketed with an earthen financial organization, developing a stroll-in root cellar.

Septic tank root cellars are endorsed because of their ease of installation, functionality to be custom designed, resistance to moisture and seepage, and espresso rate.

6. The 'Cave' Root Cellar

This form of cellar is constructed via excavating a hillside to make it look like a cave.' The cave's walls and roofs are then reinforced to make sure its structural integrity. The essential advantage of this sort of cellar is that it is self-regulating, requiring very little outside have an effect on to keep the temperature and humidity.

The downside of cave root cellars is that they may be vulnerable to immoderate climate situations and, if no longer well built, can collapse, ensuing in destruction and, in some times, even demise.

Types of root cellars encompass: above floor, conventional, and barrel-made.

Factors to Consider earlier than Choosing a Root Cellar Design

Before you choose a root cellar format for your property, maintain in mind the following factors, as they'll have an impact on the sturdiness of your food and the durability of your cellar.

1. Topography

The topography of the land you pick will assist you make a decision what form of cellar to assemble.

If your location is rocky, it's miles no longer going that you will find out a right patch of land a good way to will will permit you to dig some distance sufficient. In this case, an above-ground root cellar is your super bet.

If you select out out a place with hundreds of rain, the box kind, and the hollow-in-the-ground are your wonderful alternatives due to the truth the field's metal prevents water from seeping in.

A sloped piece of land is ideal for a cave root cellar as it permits you to without trouble dig out the shape and shape of the cellar.

2. Food to Store

While all root cellars can preserve something stored inner them, a few are better best to the task than others. Fruits and root veggies, for example, save a ways better in hole-in-the-floor cellars and earthbag cellars than in basement ones. This is because of the fact the temperature and humidity at the ones ranges are more likely to be extra stable than those in a basement, which range due to insulating gadgets, heating pads, and air conditioning.

Therefore, by way of the use of figuring out to apply a basement cellar, you can should frequently display the cellar's temperature and humidity to boom your meals's shelf life.

3. Amount of Food to Store

While most cellars can preserve an less pricey amount of produce, some can hold a long way extra. Therefore, plan your cellar's duration round the quantity of produce you want to preserve. There isn't any want to spend money on a field root cellar as a small non-farming circle of relatives except you moreover mght need it to function a bunker too.

4. Climate

The weather of your environment will cautiously impact the type and layout of your root cellar.

Root cellars can also fail to carry out their capabilities in warmness, southern climates with lots of moderate and rain if they will be now not carefully monitored.

Root cellars are ideal for meals garage in cooler, northern areas similarly from the equatorial line so long as they may be well hooked up and monitored.

five. Cost of Construction

Always keep in mind the expected charge of constructing a root cellar. You can choose out the inspiration cellar format that fine fits you based totally really in your price range and the opposite factors stated above.

Basement cellars are quite simple to collect as long as you strictly adhere to the building instructions. Depending on the scale of the sectioned part of the basement you want to apply, the constructing substances may cost a bit no more than $1,000. However, if you hire a expert, the charge can be higher, ranging amongst $1,500 and $three,000.

Hole-in-the-floor cellars are the maximum an awful lot less luxurious, costing much less than $500. Most of the cash is spent on insulating fabric (like straw) and your field.

Container root cellars are fairly highly-priced, with estimates ranging among $20,000 and $fifty 5,000. This cash covers everything, together with the field, building materials, and labor.

Septic tank root cellars rate among $8,000 and $10,000, relying on the amount and period of tanks used.

Earthbag root cellars are cheap as compared to septic tanks and concern root cellars. Including all fees, they range $3,500 to $7,000.

If you rent a expert to construct your cave root cellar, the price can variety among $12,000 and $15,000. However, the charges may be decreased to a naked minimum in case you assemble it yourself.

Note that:

The fees can also additionally range primarily based completely for your location and price of products.

Every predicted rate can be reduced in case you do maximum of the labor your self.

Building a Root Cellar

Now that you've decided on the premise cellar design you need to construct, it's time to start.

You can choose out to both:

Contact a production business enterprise to manipulate the complete undertaking: If you don't need to get your hands dirty, you could offer the task to a capable production organization so that you can have your cellar organized right away.

Start the hard work yourself: If you don't thoughts doing the art work yourself, you want to build up the materials you'll want as brief as feasible. They are as follows:

Packed Earth

Gravel

Cement

Some sand

Sacks (for earthbags)

Insulating cloth (straw, hay, foam, and Styrofoam portions)

Wire netting

Container of preference

A hygrometer

A thermometer

Wood beams (for resource)

Working gear, like a shovel, hand trowel, and head pan.

Source of water

Once you have got got were given those materials, you're prepared to start.

Step-through using-step Guide to Building the Root Cellar of Your Choice

1. Basement Root Cellar

Below is a step-by way of-step manual for building a basement root cellar.

To begin, decide the pleasant part of your basement. This location want to be a protracted manner from any source of warmth, like heating pads and furnaces.

Make effective that this vicinity is properly-ventilated. Poor air flow speeds up the deterioration of meals. A window might be perfect right proper right here.

If this phase does not have a window, you may installation a air flow tube that may be opened and closed as desired.

After you've installation your location, the following step is to insulate it. Insulation may be carried out with the aid of using padding the region with a dense foam, so one can correctly stabilize temperature. You additionally can purchase lag-filled insulating materials (a substance that doesn't behavior warmth). If this is your choice, bypass for it.

The motive of insulating is to create robust conditions on the way to assist make bigger your greens' shelf life as masses as viable.

After insulating, add a in addition layer of plastic sheet to maintain moisture and air locked inside the room.

Cover the brink of your ventilator tube with cord netting to prevent mice and other pests from coming into your cellar and destroying your products.

Install your thermometer and hygrometer at the outdoor of the basement section. This allows you to reveal the temperature and humidity without continuously starting the cellar.

Your basement root cellar is now whole. All it desires now are some shelves, crates, and exclusive garage substances to organize your objects.

2. Hole-in-the-Ground Cellar

Below is a step-with the aid of manner of-step manual for constructing a hollow-in-the-ground root cellar.

Survey your land and make sure that it does not have a immoderate-water degree, as this will significantly have an impact on your produce under sooner or later of flooding.

Choose the plot wherein the cellar can be built and begin digging. This form of cellar calls for a depth of at the least 10 feet (three meters). This is due to the fact the temperature and humidity are pretty solid at this depth, and it doesn't require a drainage machine. The width of the hole can vary counting on the scale of the sector being used.

Put the container inside the hollow you dug. If you operate a wood subject, make sure it is rot-resistant.

Styrofoam must be used to insulate your field, and a layer of the earth need to be introduced to allow for moisture.

Insulate your box's lid, taking particular care to ensure that it fits perfectly with the field.

Make a second lid just like the number one but has a tremendous peak of approximately 6 inches. This lid can be low in the floor, with little distinction from the relaxation of the earth surrounding it. It will keep water and frost off the principle lid while additionally serving as a landmark.

Your hole-in-the-floor cellar is now whole.

three. Container Root Cellar

Below is a step-with the useful resource of-step manual for constructing a discipline root cellar.

Dig a hole massive sufficient to address your area with an excavator.

Construct maintaining walls around the excavated location. This need to be finished with concrete due to the truth the partitions have to be sturdy sufficient to rise up to the strain of the earth as fast as the sector is included.

While the concrete dries, set up your drainage machine.

Lower the sector into the gap and begin filling inside the factors with earth.

Build wood beams or braces within the field to guide the burden of the earth as a way to be heaped on top of the roof.

Arrange for air waft systems to be mounted in the container as nicely. A simple example is the installation of a vent above to permit heat air to break out and some other one below at the opportunity component of the primary vent to allow cool air to enter. Remember to shut their edges with cord netting.

To hold moisture inside the cellar, insulate it with materials like Styrofoam.

Provide lights so you can find your way round while vital.

Install a thermometer and a hygrometer to display the temperature and humidity in the box.

Cover the sphere's roof with earth, spreading it lightly to lessen the weight on one thing.

Insulate the element of the door with insulating material and cowl it with a similarly layer of plastic sheet.

Container root cellars are fantastically flexible and might effects keep masses of kilos of food, wine, meats, and one-of-a-kind devices.

four. Earthbag Root Cellar

Below is a step-by using the use of-step manual for building an earthbag root cellar.

Dig out the popular area to the desired depth, keeping in thoughts that the earthbags will absorb some place as quick as organized.

Use sacks with pores for the earthbags.

You can fill the lowest half of of with stones first, discovered thru earth, or a mixture of each.

Pack the aggregate up to three/four of the sack, tie it tightly, after which beat it until it is adequately flattened.

Arrange those bags in rows to create the favored top of the cellar walls.

Use timber beams to assist any tough fabric you need for the roof. You can, for example, use strengthened steel or a awesome tarp spread over robust wiring. Finish it off with some concrete.

Insulate your roof with a Styrofoam lining and a water-evidence sheet.

Because the roof is probably the component above floor, be part of your drainage tool to the top wall and the roof sticking out.

Because the luggage perform air flow in earthbags, it could now not be vital. Still, you could set up it as a precaution, making sure that the two vents are contrary. Remember to apply cord netting to regular the ends.

Fill any exposed holes in the cellar walls with concrete, ensuring they're truely sealed.

Install your door and check for any holes that might allow rodents into your cellar.

Place a layer of earth over the now-dry concrete to absolutely seal the shape.

Things to Keep in Mind approximately Root Cellars

Below are some things to hold in thoughts while building a root cellar:

Building a cellar near a tree will make digging extraordinarily difficult. When the tree grows, its roots will crack the adjacent form.

If the moisture in your cellar is low, area a bowl of water in the center. This water can be effortlessly absorbed to be used, and any more may be expelled via the vents.

You have to high-quality preserve root veggies in hole-in-the-ground cellars due to the fact the cellar does not permit for correct air air glide, making it volatile to shop different factors.

When building your cellar, smaller bins are endorsed due to the truth they're much less tough to control in phrases of temperature and humidity than large ones.

When the cellar isn't always in use, continuously turn off the lighting fixtures. Light has been proven to turn out to be worse meals with the beneficial aid of encouraging sprouting.

If feasible, keep away from floors the ground of your cellar with some thing other than packed earth. It will act as an excellent conductor and insulator.

Root cellars are swiftly replacing fridges due to their uncanny capability to keep meals for longer durations without energy. This unmarried characteristic makes each penny you spend worthwhile.

Many root cellar designs can be hired primarily based completely to your necessities and tastes.

An underground root cellar is a famous layout that leverages the natural insulation of the soil to hold a normal temperature and humidity degree. A basement root cellar is some other opportunity, which makes use of the cold temperatures and immoderate humidity observed in most basements to keep veggies. An underground root cellar is a terrific option for folks who need to maintain vegetables and end result in a natural manner. They can be constructed using lots of substances, together with brick, stone, or concrete, and are generally dug into the floor. They are designed to take advantage of the herbal insulation of the soil to hold a constant temperature and humidity diploma, it is right for preserving end stop result and greens.

A basement root cellar is each different possibility, which makes use of the bloodless temperatures and immoderate humidity determined in most basements to hold greens. This type of root cellar is frequently built into the basement of an existing domestic and may be a price-effective and area-green way to keep produce. It's crucial to be conscious that every kinds of root cellars want right air flow to keep away from mold and mildew and need to be saved darkish to keep away from light damage to the stored produce.

An above-floor root cellar is each distinct preference that can be built with insulating substances like foam board to preserve a normal temperature. Whichever layout you pick out, make certain that the foundation cellar has enough air flow to keep away from more moisture, which may additionally moreover purpose rot. Maintain a regular temperature to hold food from deteriorating.

When designing a root cellar, keep in mind factors like place, insulation, and air float to guarantee its efficacy in retaining produce. Building a root cellar is a clever investment with a purpose to genuinely repay ultimately.

Chapter 4: Root Cellar Organization Tips

Properly storing your stop end result and veggies for your cellar preserve their vitamins and taste. One of the maximum essential secrets and techniques and strategies and strategies to a successful root cellar is enterprise and arrangement. The u.S.A. And order of your root cellar can make or wreck its basic performance.

A nicely organized cellar will guarantee that your culmination and greens live sparkling all 12 months. Even in case you aren't developing the whole lot yourself, losing stored produce will charge you a whole lot of coins. Make an try to be meticulous together along with your root cellar employer; you don't need to go through the strain of cultivating, developing, and harvesting all that produce only to waste all of it.

Many people remove their plans to construct a root cellar due to the truth they're worried approximately the organization technique and the manner tough it is able to be. Their preference and zeal to growth extra powerful techniques to consume greater healthily wane due to that, and that they revert back to their vintage routines. But that shouldn't be the case; you shouldn't need to shut the door for your hopes for a more match way of life in reality due to the fact the opportunity of retaining your root cellar neat seems daunting. Today, you'll observe a few clean strategies for making the most out of the gap you've got to be had.

You don't want a large out of doors or a spacious basement to have a cellar. If you want one, you may assemble one with the excellent materials. The fine hassle that topics is the way you put together it. You don't want a good buy coins, gadget, or possibly a plot of land to maintain up on all that herbal goodness. A difficulty, a trash can, or perhaps a small vicinity in your attic may be transformed proper right into a root cellar to shop vegetables like squash, beetroots, carrots, potatoes, sweet potatoes, and cabbage.

You may were the use of your root cellar, however it's so crowded and cluttered that you don't recognize what to do and are continuously dropping time seeking out belongings you want. You don't need to want to look for that one apple you understand is at the bottom of the stack. Don't worry—you'll take a look at everything you want to arrange your root cellar like an expert.

With the need to devour extra healthy turning into more urgent and root cellars creating a huge comeback, getting it proper is important. You ought to have a useful method for organizing your root cellar. It is more than definitely having an open area you can use for garage; you need to realize in which the entirety belongs and the manner great to store topics. Customizing your place will let you store extra and use your area properly.

This bankruptcy will educate you a way to use your shelves, drawers, and containers. You will find out a manner to make the most of your root cellar. You'll study in which to start and a way to decide which storage options are great for you and whether or not or no longer you require drawers, numerous types of cabinets, bins, or a particular vicinity for every form of meals. Once you've determined that, it's time to start sorting!

Understanding Root Cellar Storage Options

There are remarkable alternatives for organizing a root cellar. The enterprise fashion is determined via the available location and the kinds of culmination and vegetables you choice to hold and preserve.

Before you begin arranging and organizing, make an intensive listing of the containers you'll be the usage of and the shelving you'll want for the quit result and veggies you'll be storing; this will placed matters into mind-set and make the method an lousy lot less difficult. You want to moreover make a listing of critical root cellar devices like mesh luggage, sand, and hooks on your walls or cabinets.

Shelves are the most commonplace manner to hold food in a root cellar. You can each purchase cabinets or construct them yourself. Keep comparable factors collectively even as the usage of cabinets. Keep all your potatoes or all of your onions collectively, as an instance. This will help you hold tune of what you've got and make rotating your food a lot much less difficult.

Drawers are each different opportunity. This is useful when you have lots of additives or if you need that allows you to see the whole lot at a look. It's furthermore a extremely good desire when you have restricted region on your root cellar. You can also shop your food in boxes. This is a superb alternative if you need to preserve things organized or if you're short on area. Make nice that the packing containers are watertight and that the meals is well sealed.

How to Organize a Root Cellar

Now that you recognise how a root cellar works, it's time to check the strategies involved in organizing it.

1. Utilizing Drawers, Shelves, and Containers

Using drawers, shelves, and packing containers is one of the first-class techniques to maximize your root cellar area. Drawers are awesome for preserving smaller gadgets like herbs, onions, and potatoes organized. Larger gadgets, like canned goods or jars, may be saved on shelves with easy plastic baskets or bins.

Keeping matters organized will make it less complicated to speedy discover what you need. You also can separate components with the beneficial useful resource of type and maintain them in categorized bins. You'll continuously apprehend what's in each container and can without problem discover what you're looking for this manner.

2. Keeping Similar Foods Together

Similar elements need to be saved collectively on the identical time as organizing your root cellar. This makes it a great deal much less difficult to discover what you're seeking out and cuts down on the time you spend wandering round. It not best makes it much less complicated to find items but moreover saves region and preserves your end quit end result and greens due to the reality first-class saved merchandise can not be stored together. They can interfere with each other's taste or shelf existence. Apples are one such item that want to be stored separate to your root cellar. If you need to ripen it, place it with different end end result like persimmons or avocados. Apples produce and incorporate the most ethylene, that would purpose spoilage of different ethylene-touchy devices like asparagus, squash, broccoli, pumpkins, cauliflower, carrot, onions, Brussels sprouts, cucumbers, lettuce, and wonderful leafy greens. Mangoes, bananas, avocados, honeydews, pears, peaches, potatoes, plums, strawberries, and tomatoes are a number of the opportunity ethylene-producing culmination and veggies. They must no longer be stored with ethylene-touchy culmination and veggies.

Knowing which components are ethylene-producing and which might be ethylene-sensitive is important to having a a achievement root cellar. That is what will assist you decide what must and shouldn't go together with what. Keep that during mind will help your produce very last longer.

There are also an entire lot of different options. Foods can be labeled consistent with their type (veggies and culmination), season, or use (cooking or canning). You also can use severa types of shelves and boxes that will help you live organized.

Consider the numerous styles of meals you'll be storing and enterprise them as a result. For instance, root vegetables like onions and garlic may be stored collectively, as can fruit like apples and pears. Herbs like parsley and cilantro can also be mixed.

If you're unsure in which to start, have a look at your grocery list and be aware which devices you regularly buy together. You should be capable of discover an area for them for your root cellar.

Whatever tool you select out, be everyday. That manner, you'll constantly apprehend in which to go to get the food you require.

three. Keeping a Journal

Keep a mag of what you're storing on your root cellar and at the same time as it have come to be harvested even as you're first starting. This will help you keep song of what's on your cellar and on the same time because it'll expire. This is specifically essential while storing perishable items like give up end result and greens.

Keeping a magazine is one of the most effective and most inexperienced processes to put together your root cellar. It lets in you to keep tune of what you put in every bin or drawer similarly to the date it emerge as stored. By the usage of that information, you may be able to correctly rotate meals gadgets and avoid having to dig through the whole lot to find that one jar of pickles you put in last year. It's additionally an remarkable manner to song what you need and dislike. If you have got a specifically a achievement harvest, write it all of the way all the way down to your mag so that you can reflect it the subsequent season. Or, if some thing does now not pass as deliberate, you may avoid it the subsequent time.

Finally, preserving a mag of what you have got for your root cellar will will can help you hold tune of what has been used and what wishes to be grew to emerge as around. This will will let you recognise what you want to inventory up on and what you have were given loads of. Include what is going in which on your root cellar, as well as what is going at the shelf, drawer, or jar. You can also consist of factors just like the date of garage, what objects are stored, the sort of numerous produce saved, how plenty they rate, wherein they had been purchased, whether they were from a farm or the marketplace if you got them, similarly to some distinctive information you discovered is applicable and well worth noting.

4. Rotating Food for Longevity

When making plans your root cellar, endure in thoughts that you'll want a gadget to rotate food so that they're used on time. It can be tremendous if you had a plan for rotating meals gadgets for your root cellar. This manner you've got to analyze your meals frequently and eat the oldest produce first. Keep tune of what desires to be used first with the resource of storing gadgets steady with their expiration date.

When saved nicely, most root veggies will very last several weeks, if not extra than a month. On the opposite hand, starchy greens have a shelf existence of only some weeks.

Foods need for use within the order of shortest shelf lifestyles to longest shelf existence. Older elements need to be moved to the the the front of the cabinets so that not something receives misplaced inside the decrease decrease again. If you can maintain a magazine to your root cellar detailing what's saved and while it grow to be delivered, you'll be able to effortlessly communicate to it at the same time as you want to transport subjects spherical or get an concept of what wants to be eaten or replenished first.

Keep some "tricks" or suggestions in mind to make rotating and monitoring meals plenty less hard. For example, you could separate meals into 3 classes: "Eat now - These want for use proper away!", "Eat soon - These will hold within the root cellar for 2 weeks or much less," and "Use later - These can stay in the root cellar for up to as a minimum one month". Then, make a chart with expiration dates and type your gadgets subsequently.

Store comparable gadgets together, like potatoes with potatoes and carrots with carrots, for longer-term food storage. This manner, any spoilage can be contained, and matters received't spoil faster due to incorrect grouping. By taking this simple step, the entirety stays sparkling till you need it!

Finally, label all boxes, drawers, and shelves with their contents so that you recognize precisely what's wherein. With this organizational device, you could without trouble take inventory of what dreams for use first and decrease waste.

five. Maintaining the Perfect Temperature

It is vital to keep your root cellar at the best temperature. For example, fruits, greens, and dairy products should be saved at precise temperatures. The maximum critical detail is to recognize the way to adjust humidity and temperature based totally on the type of products you're storing.

The ideal temperature variety for root cellars is 32°F to forty°F (or zero°C to four.Five°C), and the best humidity variety is ninety – 90 5%. For meals to be well-preserved, those factors ought to be saved in stability. Keep an eye fixed on the moisture ranges in your root cellar and warm things up with a small heater if it will become damp or cold. Remember to preserve the doorways closed as a splendid deal as possible to keep a everyday temperature in the root cellar.

Arranging Your Root Cellar

Here are a few mind for installing your root cellar preceding to arranging it:

1. Choose the proper area: A root cellar must be buried or in issue underground, with a north-coping with wall to help with temperature manage.

2. Insulate the walls: If you insulate the partitions of your root cellar, the temperature will stay robust, and you won't must use as an awful lot warmth or air con. To protect the partitions, use substances like foam insulation or straw bales.

three. Proper air glide: Proper air flow is essential for regulating the temperature and humidity in the root cellar. Allow for air motion with the resource of installing vents at the pinnacle and backside of the basement.

four. Store food properly: Proper food storage is vital for extending the shelf existence of your stored food. Vegetables need to be saved in hermetic boxes, like boxes or baskets, in choice to at the floor—save quit bring about a fab, dry place on cabinets or inside the rafters in a unmarried layer.

5. Use a thermometer: To assure that the temperature in your root cellar remains regular, use a thermometer. Most fruits and veggies have to be stored at a temperature of 32-forty°F.

6. Keep it clean: Clean the muse cellar frequently to prevent dirt and vermin from accumulating.

7. Label and cycle your meals: Mark all your root cellar food with the date it changed into added. This will make rotating your food and the usage of the oldest products first masses plenty less complex.

Tips and Tricks for Organizing a Root Cellar

Here are a few famous employer hints and suggestions to get you began out. These tips will help your root cellar be successful and have you ever consuming like a king right away.

Packing your root greens in damp sand or sawdust will help them ultimate longer. This is specifically useful in extraordinarily dry cellars. Make certain it's surely damp, now not soggy, that it starts offevolved offevolved to sprout or rot.

Keep your root cellar cool at some stage in harvesting and storing intervals.

Keep crates and containers suspended to allow air to circulate across the greens or stop quit result inner.

Store squash and pumpkins with out their stems.

Only keep your super produce; do no longer hassle retaining objects which can be beaten, bruised, insect-broken, or displaying signs and symptoms and signs of spoilage.

Before storing your nuts in an airtight jar, make certain that they will be honestly dry.

Garlic, squash, onions, and pumpkins need to not be saved in damp regions.

Avoid storing end result and greens in big piles or mounds; maintain them in small piles for your cellar.

Put clear labels in your jars, containers, and crates to beautify accessibility.

Handle all produce you want to preserve with excessive care.

When packing your leafy greens for garage, lessen decrease once more the leafy tops of veggies with the aid of way of the usage of round an inch.

Vegetables should in no way be left or stored on naked concrete or tiled flooring.

Make quality that your root cellar has right enough air glide.

Importance of Organizing Your Root Cellar

Organizing your root cellar is vital to taking complete gain of the talents and advantages it has to provide. With a right plan, you could maximize to be had region, maintain comparable devices grouped for tons much less complex get entry to, and speedy discover out-of-location gadgets.

First, set apart a few drawers or shelves to interrupt up prevent quit end result and greens. Different cabinets may be installation depending on the form of meals being saved; twine racks are first-rate for heavier gadgets like canned objects. In assessment, mild-weight devices like potatoes or onions may be located on flat surfaces.

There are numerous certainly one of a kind advantages to properly organizing your root cellar. Keeping a written inventory of the entirety in your cellar allows you to make certain that every one of your materials have emerge as used on time. Nothing will destroy due to overcrowding or flawed storage via retaining comparable foods together, rotating your food shares, and along with drawers, cabinets, and boxes to better save your objects.

A well-organized root cellar moreover permits you to find out what you want whilst favored. It may be a breeze to fast grasp what is needed without rummaging thru piles of meals or root veggies with an organized setup and smooth-to-observe labels. This will save on every occasion and frustration!

A properly-prepared root cellar is likewise an vital issue of keeping your stored produce glowing and available. You can use shelving or bins to keep your give up result and veggies separate and without trouble identifiable. It is likewise a exquisite concept to apply clean packing containers or jars to will let you see the contents with out starting them. Clear plastic bins also are useful because of the fact they may will let you see the contents with out starting up them. Labeling your packing containers with the date and contents is likewise a amazing idea. This manner, you can keep song of ways long your produce has been saved and rotate them consequently. A properly-prepared root cellar makes it easy to discover what you need whilst you need it.

It will take a few trial and errors, much like some thing else, to parent out what works remarkable for you and your cellar. However, with a little attempt, you need to create a handy storage place that keeps your meals glowing and delicious. Always don't forget to maintain your garage place properly-ventilated and at a consistent temperature. It's additionally an extremely good concept to research your root cellar each few weeks for spoilage or other problems, so that you can restock with sparkling gadgets as wanted. With these forms of tips in thoughts, organizing your root cellar need to be a breeze!

Chapter 5: What to Store in a Root Cellar

A root cellar is a traditional food preservation approach. We want to all embody it due to the fact it is able to save a huge kind of culmination and greens.

Before refrigeration, storing beets, turnips, potatoes, carrots, parsnips, and different root greens required an underground root cellar. Root cellars are gaining recognition yet again as a way to keep meals from freezing within the wintry weather and funky within the summer time to prevent it from spoiling.

Conditions for Root Cellars

To make sure that your gift or new root cellar meets requirements, you'll need to apprehend what constitutes a true root cellar:

It ought to be evidence in competition to humidity ranges of eighty 5-90 five% and temperatures starting from 32 to forty tiers Fahrenheit. Because of this, it will no longer typically art work in warmth climates.

Root cellars are not authorised close to septic structures or areas with a excessive water table.

You have to be capable of control the temperature, air float, drainage, and humidity.

Before beginning any production, test together with your nearby building department to look if there are any functionality prison necessities.

By carefully thinking about the precise flora you choose out out, your harvest time frame, and the proper garage necessities for every form of vegetable or fruit, you can use a root cellar to revel in summer season flavors inside the wintry weather.

When root cellaring, maintain food as easy as possible and cope with it with care. Whether you purchase produce in bulk from the farmer's marketplace or acquire it from your lawn, very well check out the food to make certain that it is rotting or beginning to damage.

There are large varieties of perishable food: produce that shops properly in cold and damp situations and one which desires to be stored at a slightly hotter and drier temperature. The produce in every list need to be organized by way of the use of temperature choice, with brought statistics on great practices for harvesting, storage, and prolonged-lasting sorts.

Consult the county cooperative extension table to tailor your root cellar plans to your particular place. They can recommend you at the outstanding garage alternatives on your area and supply an motive for any weather-associated troubles you can stumble upon.

Where and Why do People use Root Cellars?

Anyone can assemble a root cellar to preserve their plant life stored and geared up to use if they need a place to save their meals. Fruits, veggies, and other components can be saved on shelves to keep them smooth till desired.

Root cellars are beneficial for individuals who increase their very very personal food due to the truth they turn them right into a wonderful funding at the way to keep all of their produce after harvest.

The Benefits of Root Cellars

Even no matter the truth that root vegetables aren't specially pricey, the fee of a homegrown beet or potato is some distance superior. Grocery shops don't usually inventory greens all three hundred and sixty five days (otherwise you come to be looking for an out-of-season and unappealing vegetable!).

Furthermore, excellent sufficient meals safety without reliance on supermarkets or capability deliver chain disruptions offers heaps-wanted peace of thoughts.

In desired, root cellars are an brilliant funding for folks who enlarge and hold a big amount of food all twelve months.

The following are the pinnacle benefits of root cellars:

Food super and safety

Additional storage

Minimal protection and power necessities

Reduces fees

Reduces the charge of crop decay

Eco-first-class and sustainable

The very last benefit is that because the foundation cellar's temperature will absolutely cool or refrigerate the produce for you, you obtained't should pay as loads for electricity.

Root Cellar for Storing Vegetables

Below are some of the topics that you can hold in your root cellar.

1. Root Vegetables

Some people like to go away veggies like beef, turnips, and carrots in the lawn for so long as possible, mulched with straw, because of the reality they taste even better after a frost.

Before the floor freezes, you can nonetheless dig them up and skip them to the foundation cellar for bloodless, wet garage. Brush away the leafy tops and any more soil.

The fantastic way to hold root vegetables is to layer them in a box with soil or damp sawdust. Another technique that works properly is straw layers packed inner a five-gallon plastic bucket.

2. Leafy Vegetables

Leafy veggies like kale, Chinese cabbage, and cabbage could have their roots eliminated from the garden. Don't fear about removing all of the soil; definitely brush it away. It is last that you replant leafy greens within the root cellar soil, perhaps in a hollow or a big basin.

However, by way of way of eliminating any decaying exterior leaves and storing the cabbage on a slatted rack inside the root cellar, you may be capable of preserve head cabbage and Chinese cabbage for some months. Low temperatures and immoderate humidity are best garage situations for leafy greens.

three. Leeks, Onions, and Garlic

Leeks, which can be related to onions, hold properly in root cellars. Cover your garden with a thick layer of mulch in advance than a tough frost. They want to then be dug up whilst no matter the truth that intact.

Some gardeners choose to leave the leeks by myself, covered in a thick layer of mulch.

To save the leeks, region them in a huge bucket. They keep pleasant at a low temperature of 32 to 40°F and a excessive humidity stage of ninety to ninety 5%.

If harvesting leeks isn't always feasible due to frozen floor, get rid of them from the lawn, replant them in a shallow bathtub, or store them to your cellar with soil at the roots.

Compared to your leafy veggies and root vegetables, onions, and garlic choose a hotter, an awful lot much less humid surroundings; intention for a temperature of 50°F and a humidity of about 50%.

Design your root cellar throughout the wishes of your plant life, which encompass an antechamber that regulates warmness (in the summer season, it's hotter than the interior, and inside the winter, it's colder). This lets in you to maintain some vegetation within the indoors area and others outside. However, some people like to hold garlic and onions reachable of their houses. Wrap the rope across the onions and braid the garlic for smooth garage.

4. Potatoes

Potatoes are some of the top notch flora to grow and maintain. However, storing potatoes harvested in the early summer time may be hard.

If storage situations are too warm for potatoes harvested in July, they may sprout. Grow a 2d crop or perhaps a later crop harvested inside the fall if you want to shop potatoes for the wintry climate.

Potatoes which have been cured will stay in a very cold but not freezing environment for months. Cure potatoes in a temperature and humidity-controlled surroundings for 1-2 weeks. Then store them on your root cellar.

It is suggested to store your potatoes in subsurface depth to keep away from rot signs and symptoms. These vegetable garage rack containers are nice for storing potatoes.

Because in their high sensitivity to slight, potatoes need to be stored in a darkish place.

Some people experience using straws to cowl their potato packing containers.

five. Squash

Root cellars are generally too humid and cold for squash. Instead, most humans preserve wintry weather squash in their mudroom, that's typically the satisfactory part of the house. With a temperature of 65 levels Fahrenheit, it's far right for iciness squash.

6. Apples

Because apples require bloodless temperatures, preferably amongst 32 and 40 degrees Fahrenheit and 90 to ninety five percent humidity, storing them in a root cellar may be difficult.

Tart apples final longer than candy apples, and heirloom apple types outperform extra contemporary ones. Some of the satisfactory apples to hold in a root cellar are:

Arbuckle Black

Criterion

Honeycrisp

Red Lady

Beauty of Rome

Only ripe, spotless apples ought to be stored, and every one need to be for my part wrapped in newspaper. Then, place the blanketed apples in a cardboard subject or a wooden fruit crate for storage.

For the splendid outcomes, each apple should be in my opinion wrapped earlier than being placed interior a timber fruit crate.

7. Cabbages

Don't be too concerned about cleaning cabbage. In a certainly perfect international, you'd go away the roots by myself and replant them inside the root cellar soil. This is most effective to do in a massive basin, like a trash can.

Another desire is to bundle each cabbage head one after the alternative and stack them on a shelf with some location among them.

Above all, do no longer depart the cabbage out within the open because the scent will permeate the concept cellar and dilute the flavor of apples, pears, and celery.

eight. Sweet Potatoes

Root cellars are an obvious desire for the amazing majority of root plant life. Only undamaged, unblemished sweet potatoes need to be harvested inside the late fall for prolonged-term garage.

Remove any extra soil and allow it to treatment for 5 to ten days in humid situations amongst 80 and eighty five stages F.

After curing, store the potatoes in a dry location with temperatures no decrease than 55°F and humidity stages amongst 60 and 70%. Make top notch the field wherein the sweet potatoes are saved is nicely-ventilated.

9. Carrots

Carrots left at the soil floor after a moderate frost are the superb. It's extraordinary to keep them within the lawn for as long as viable. You can cover them with straw.

You'll want to get them earlier than the floor freezes. Have you ever attempted extracting carrots from frozen ground? It's not superb.

Carrots want to be saved for your root cellar at a temperature of 33 to 40°F and a humidity stage of 90 to 90 5%.

10. Beets

Beets are root vegetables which could withstand bloodless temperatures starting from 32 to forty degrees Fahrenheit as well as immoderate humidity stages beginning from 90 to ninety 5 percentage. They need to be harvested at the identical time because the roots are about 2 inches significant and the weather is dry.

Beets ought to be dug up, and their tops must be removed, but they want to be left intact for one to two inches. The root tip need to moreover be left linked.

After harvesting the beets, disregard any loose soil and cowl them with sawdust, damp sand, or peat moss.

The beets should no longer come into contact with each amazing because of the reality this increases the possibility of spoilage.

11. Pears

Like apples, pears ought to be stored in a root cellar at cold temperatures. They thrive in temperatures beginning from 33 to forty degrees Fahrenheit and relative humidity degrees starting from 80 to 90%.

Each pear should be wrapped in newspaper in advance than being located in a cardboard or wooden box with plastic wrap on top. They need to be saved at the decrease shelves of the basis cellar. Only keep end result which can be best and free of bruises.

Pears can be difficult to preserve in a root cellar because of the reality they will be temperature touchy and should be stored at the coldest temperatures. Avoid placing them near greens that produce ethylene gas, and use them up within months.

12. Pumpkins

Homesteaders and settlers used to keep pumpkins for the wintry climate. But they weren't most effective for pies.

Harvest your pumpkins in advance than the primary frost, ensuring that at the least an inch of the stem stays intact. Pumpkins that don't have a stem are much more likely to rot.

Cure at 80-80 5 stages Fahrenheit for ten days. Pumpkins preserve exceptional in temperatures starting from forty to 50 levels Fahrenheit and relative humidity stages beginning from 60 to 70%. Almost any squash can be stored in this manner.

thirteen. Parsnips

They have to be saved at immoderate humidity stages of 90 to ninety five percent and temperatures of 33 to forty °F.

Parsnips, like carrots, may be left within the lawn blanketed in the mulch. The trouble is that parsnips dislike the herbal thawing and freezing cycles that arise when they may be left within the garden beds. Keeping parsnips in a root cellar is a wise desire.

Remove the tops, layer them with moist sand or peat moss interior a box, and near the container.

14. Broccoli

Although broccoli does now not preserve for extended, it's miles at its outstanding while saved at 32 °F (carefully regulated) with a immoderate moisture content material material. Trim them and location them in perforated plastic bags.

Avoid storing ethylene-emitting produce, like apples, for your storage area because it will notably reduce the tremendous of broccoli.

Try to constantly pass for Greenbelt, Legacy, Marathon, Green Comet, Waltham 29, and Marathon versions.

15. Brussels Sprouts

For the high-quality flavor, harvest brussels sprouts after many frosty touches. If you have got vicinity, you can repot the plant, dangle it inverted from the roots, or keep it all for your cellar earlier than harvesting.

If you don't have an lousy lot area, choose the plantlets and vicinity them in a porous plastic bag.

16. Beans (Dried)

Allow the beans to mature on the plant till they rattle. The whole plant want to be eliminated and dried for a further one to 2 weeks in a safe, shaded vicinity.

If your thumbnail leaves a electricity at the pods, permit them to dry for longer. Then, hand-beat seedlings in competition to a organisation ground or shell. Before storing in a sealed jar, chaff need to be eliminated with an air compressor or hair dryer.

Some growers defrost uncooked beans for several weeks to kill weevils. For storage, use an hermetic container.

Some of the great sorts encompass Adzuki, Black Coco, Jacobs' Cattle, Brown Dutch, Speckled Cranberry, Tiger's Eye (Repokeb), Steuben, and Yin Yang.

17. Jerusalem Artichoke

These tubers preserve better within the floor than in a root cellar; if the floor does no longer freeze, they may be left in the garden all wintry climate.

When exposed to freezing or near-freezing temperatures, their starches degrade over the years, converting their colour, texture, and taste. Tubers which may be ill, broken, or skinned will damage faster.

Fuseau is the maximum commonplace range, but Corlis Bolton Haynes is a lesser-acknowledged heirloom variety that also flourishes in colder climates.

18. Tomatillos

When the papery husk splits or turns from green to tan, it's time to reap.

Store inner a netted bag, basket, or paper bag in a dry, properly-ventilated place. Tomatillos keep fantastic of their husks; however, inside the event that they show signs of mould, peel and wash them earlier than storing them inside the fridge.

According to many seed stores, purple tomatillos closing longer than Verde.

Guidelines for Stashing Root Cellar Vegetables

Seeing the manner you spent months cultivating veggies on your lawn, you need to make certain that your harvest is properly stored. Here are some hints for having the best revel in possible even as storing in a root cellar:

1.   When stocking the cellar later within the growing season, don't forget refrigerating the greens and end result first.

2.   Various veggies, which embody onions, wintry weather squash, potatoes, and pumpkins, need to be cured before being stored in a root cellar. Curing takes place in heat environments.

3.   Instead of washing away free dirt, brush it away. Excess moisture have to be prevented at the equal time as storing veggies and fruits in root cellars as it promotes rot.

4.   Vegetables need to be dealt with carefully to keep away from bruising, which leads to decomposition.

5.   Apples and pears are end result that emit ethylene gas. These stop give up result ought to be wrapped in paper to prevent rotting.

6.   Give the vegetables a few space on the cabinets. When they may be too close to each unique, they generate warmth, which reasons spoilage.

7. Vegetables to your root cellar ought to be checked frequently, and any symptoms and signs and symptoms of rot must prompt their elimination. Fruits and veggies rot quicker because of the gasses.

eight. Using strain-treated wood or building a root cellar in a storage isn't recommended.

9. Vegetables piled excessive generate warm temperature, which can motive spoilage. Vegetables ought to be gently allotted on cabinets near the floor. The cabinets must be rotated often.

10. Check your greens often and discard any that display signs of rot. The proverb "One awful apple ruins the complete barrel" originates from classes found in the root cellar.

How to Maintain a Cool Root Cellar

Consider the subsequent guidelines to beautify the surroundings on your root cellar:

The temperature need to be sturdy at round 10 ft (3 meters).

Avoid digging a root cellar near a big tree because of the reality the roots will in the end spread and weaken the cellar partitions.

Because wooden conducts warm temperature and cold extra slowly than steel, wood structures, packing containers, and shelving want to be used inner.

Shelves need to be positioned one to 3 toes (three to 8 cm) far from the partitions to permit for air go together with the drift, that's important for reducing airborne mold.

Packed earth is the tremendous flooring for open-air root cellars. Cement works properly and is smart for a cellar internal a basement.

Every root cellar need to have a thermometer and a hygrometer to diploma temperature and humidity. These gadgets should be checked day by day.

An exhaust pipe or a air drift device is normally used to manipulate heat, usually via way of way of allowing cold air to go into and decrease the temperature, mainly on cold fall nights.

Is Ventilation Necessary in a Root Cellar?

Ventilation is wanted in root cellars. Failure to offer adequate air go with the flow is the severa most commonplace errors whilst designing a root cellar. Food stored without this may harm.

Several veggies produce and emit ethylene gasoline, which influences nearby produce and accelerates the ripening gadget. Several of those gasses can get away thru air go with the flow. For that cause, you want to allow some of the humidity out. Otherwise, you'll danger having mildew.

A variety of things have an impact on how prolonged veggies and quit result stay glowing in root cellars, in conjunction with:

Earlier or later plants (late-maturing plants have a propensity to save higher)

Conditions for storage (an lousy lot much less-than-superb shorten storage existence)

Fruit and vegetable exceptional while saved (proper curing of damage-unfastened produce outcomes in longer garage existence).

Chapter 6: Harvesting and Preparing

With a root cellar, you can experience the bounty of summer time well into the wintry climate if you pay near hobby to the crop kinds you choose out, the harvest time, and the maximum green storage situations for each fruit or vegetable.

This financial disaster will teach you the way to harvest, prepare, and keep various fruits and greens in a root cellar.

Beets

When and the way you harvest beets will depend on wherein and when they were planted, the community climate, and the preferred trends of your beet crop. As a cool-season crop, spring and fall are the most useful seasons for growing beets in most regions.

When and How to Harvest Beets

Most species mature among fifty 5 and 70 days after planting. You need to cause for a - month harvest window after planting beets.

The pinnacle of the road temperature variety for beets is among 60 and sixty five °F (15 and 18 °C).

If beets are grown in an surroundings with a consistent daylight hours temperature above 80 °F (26 °C), their growth is probably stunted, and their taste will reduce.

In regions with mild winters and well-worn-out soil, beets ought to be left inside the floor as long as feasible.

To harvest, cautiously dig spherical and underneath the growing beets, taking care no longer to rip them and put off them from the soil.

After lifting the roots, twist the vegetables off. The storage lifestyles can be extensively improved if the caps are removed earlier than storing.

How to Store Beets

In a basement or cellar, you can keep beets smooth for up to three months, it is an tremendous desire in case you want to save a big amount. This method is typically used by individuals who develop their very very personal beets.

The quality beets should be stored, even as broken or bruised ones have a brief shelf existence and need to be ate up right now. They must be lightly brushed to dispose of soil in advance than being stored.

Avoid washing in advance than storage; ensure that they'll be sincerely dry.

Maintain a root cellar temperature of 32-40 ° F and a humidity of 90 5%.

Before storing the beets, get rid of the stems and leaves.

To preserve beets wet, location them in a massive box with a lid, together with a rubbish can, or cowl them with moist compost, sawdust, or peat moss.

Keep the compost, moss, or dust damp.

Broccoli

Broccoli want to be harvested before the florets open at the identical time because the heads are however inexperienced and organisation.

Broccoli's flower-like heads resemble bouquets. The flowers are organized for harvest 10 to 13 weeks after planting, and the flora maintain to produce buds for a similarly 6 to 8 weeks.

When and How to Harvest Broccoli

Plan your broccoli planting a very good way to be harvested sooner or later of the cool season. The finest time to plant is for the duration of late summer time and fall. Buds will open at temperatures of eighty°F (26°C) and above.

Broccoli is ready to be harvested whilst the heads are dark green and dotted with tiny, cautiously spaced buds.

After the primary head has been harvested, the secondary branches will keep developing. When issue shoots are company, they need to be harvested.

To avoid destructive the stem, reduce with sharp scissors or a knife.

Although the detail branches are possibly to supply greater open or growing heads than the applicable stem, they may be though similarly tasty.

How to Store Broccoli

Broccoli doesn't ultimate very extended, however it stores splendid at 32 °F (properly controlled) with quite a few moisture. Trim and area in a perforated plastic bag.

Store a long way far from quit end result and greens that emit ethylene gas, together with apples and tomatoes, as this could significantly lessen their shelf existence.

The length of storage is amongst 1 and a pair of weeks.

Cabbage

Cabbage is high in nutrients and an top notch supply of vitamins. It is a leafy vegetable that may be included into numerous dishes.

When and How to Harvest Cabbage

Typically, your plant may be prepared for harvest 60 to 90 days after planting. If you planted in early spring, you may harvest in late summer season.

Your cabbage plant is prepared to be harvested even as the whole head is robust.

Press firmly on the top of the pinnacle together together together with your finger. If it wiggles, leave it in the floor for a while longer.

Trim the stalk at its lowest factor at the same time as maintaining the outer, free leaves.

It is ready for intake when the leaves are tightly curled and actually hard.

Avoid leaving harvested plants exposed to the solar or rain, and harvest throughout the cooler hours of the day, specifically within the morning.

How to Store Cabbage

During summer season:

The roots and heads of cabbage plants have to be stored in a root cellar within the route of the summer season so that you may be preserved.

Place the cabbage flowers in rows on racks separated by way of using a few inches, suspend them from the ceiling with a wire, or shop them at the ground blanketed with more than one layers of newspaper.

During wintry climate:

When the floor is frozen, and snow has protected the storage pit you dug, region the cabbage roots up and the cabbage heads down, then cowl them with extra straw and a jute sack or sheet. When you want cabbage heads in the course of the iciness, definitely get rid of one from garage, stuff it with straw, and cover it.

Do no longer wash or remove the outer leaves of the cabbage before storing it. The biggest heads are folks that have been plucked whilst despite the fact that encased in their outer leaves. Handle heads with care to prevent bruising.

Cabbage will remain sparkling for 3 to four months while saved in a cool, moist environment.

Remove any heads of cabbage that begin to expose yellow or emit a rotten scent.

Carrots

If your soil is dense or difficult to art work with, you can make bigger quick styles of carrots to get the maximum at harvest time.

When and How to Harvest Carrots

Usually, more younger flora are equipped for harvest 50 to 60 days after planting.

Mature carrots require greater weeks and are normally geared up in approximately 75 days. Most carrots are prepared to be harvested even as their shoulders degree half of of of an inch to three-quarters of an inch (1.5 to two cm) in diameter.

A lawn fork may be used to loosen the soil in advance than harvesting carrots. Trim the green tops with the resource of the use of 14 – 12 inches (6–12 mm) earlier than storing.

Carrots can spend a similarly four weeks or longer in the soil sooner or later of the winter. Gather the final carrots in advance than the soil freezes. Consider what number of carrots you can eat indoors 2 to four weeks on the same time as determining at the same time as to gain them.

How to Store Carrots

Carrots, like many root plant life, can be saved inside the garden wherein they had been at the begin planted if you could cover them thoroughly with 1-2 toes of hay or straw.

Harvest your flowers at the give up of the growing season, truely in advance than the ground freezes, and maintain them indoors. If the fronds (carrot leaves) are not eliminated, they deprive the plant of water and vitamins, which reduces shelf life.

Remove the carrots' tops by way of trimming or snapping them off through hand. In a container, layer carrots with moist sand, peat, or moss.

They may be stored for four to 6 months or longer, counting on the variety and surroundings.

Pears

Pears are tremendous and some of the excellent seasonal cease quit result. Depending on the range, pears may be harvested at severa instances of the year. Early sorts are organized as a good deal as a month in advance than past due blooming types.

When and How to Harvest Pears

First, have a look at a few culmination to decide within the occasion that they have reached adulthood. Once they have fallen from the tree, pears that have not reached their complete adulthood diploma will now not be able to produce the critical sugars.

Carefully eliminate a pear from its branch using your hand. If the fruit peels with out troubles, it is ready for intake. Recalcitrant ones want to be left at the tree so that it will increase similarly.

The texture and colour of the fruit will fluctuate counting on the range, making it difficult to determine whilst to start harvesting pears genuinely via searching them.

How to Store Pears

Grow pears which can be appropriate for wintry climate storage.

Use or discard any fruit that has been damaged.

Line a discipline with 2 to three layers of cardboard and thoroughly wrap each pear on a sheet of paper.

Arrange pear packing containers neatly at the cabinets of your root cellar (do now not keep them at the floor).

Keep the temperature of the garage area among 32°F-forty°F and the relative humidity amongst 80-90%.

To prevent the relaxation of your fruit from spoiling, take a look at your pears frequently and dispose of any which may be ripe or have spots.

Pears and special prevent end result need to not be saved with greens. The ethylene gas produced through manner of end result can also reduce the shelf lifestyles of greens.

Parsnips

This root vegetable flourishes in subfreezing temperatures for about 2 to 4 weeks in the path of the cool season. During iciness, the parsnip's starch transforms into sugar, resulting in a taste this is intensely sweet and nutty.

When and How to Harvest Parsnips

Since parsnips take about 4 months (a hundred-one hundred twenty days) to mature, many gardeners depart them in the floor over the iciness.

Once the parsnip roots have completely advanced, they will be prepared for harvesting.

Keep music of while you plant your seeds so you recognize kind of while to achieve them.

Knowing how and on the identical time as to obtain a parsnip root may be beneficial as soon as your parsnips have reached adulthood. Root greens including parsnips need to be harvested nicely, as damaged or broken roots do no longer keep well.

To start, trim all the parsnip's leaves to 1 inch (2.Five cm) from the roots. Using a easy spading fork, eliminate the roots with care.

Expect a root period of 8–12 inches (20–31 cm) and a diameter of one to two inches (2.Five-five cm).

How to Store Parsnips

As with carrots, parsnips may be left in the lawn subsequently of repeated freeze-thaw cycles if a thick layer of mulch protects them.

Cut off the tops and location them in a subject with wet sand, peat, or sphagnum moss.

The garage duration is amongst 1 to two months.

Onions

Onions are a famous cool-season vegetable that may be grown from seeds, cuttings, or transplants.

Your functionality to reap onions efficiently depends on how well you plant and have a propensity to them throughout the growing season.

When and How to Harvest Onions

When the tops of inexperienced onions gain a height of six inches, they must be harvested. The green tops end up more sturdy as harvesting isn't on time.

Bulbs that have commenced to bolt or shape flower stalks want to be harvested and used proper away; they can't be saved.

When onion tops in reality fall over and turn brown, they may be harvested. Depending at the range, this commonly takes region 90 to 100 twenty days after planting.

Onions are satisfactory harvested at dawn or nightfall at the same time as the temperature is cooler.

Onions want to be cautiously dug or pulled from the soil with their tops intact. Gently shake the soil throughout the bulbs.

How to Store Onions

Onions have to be dried on paper, a show display, or hardware fabric in a dry, properly-ventilated location for 10 to fourteen days or until the skins are papery and the roots are dry.

After trimming onion tops, keep them in vented bins. Avoid the use of plastic storage bins and bags that are not permeable to air.

Sprouting takes vicinity if situations are not sufficiently dry; otherwise, storage life is prolonged.

The duration of garage degrees among five and eight months.

Pumpkins

Start with the beneficial aid of analyzing every pumpkin's rind, also called the pores and pores and skin, to decide whether or not it is harvestable. You'll want to make certain the pumpkin is the correct shade counting on the variety you're growing.

You need to furthermore observe the peel's firmness. This may be executed with the useful resource of setting a nail (or each other object) into the pumpkin's peels; if the object pierces the pores and skin without difficulty or leaves an indentation, it is however unripe.

When and How to Harvest Pumpkins

Using a hand pruner, sever the vine (an first rate knife may additionally paintings).

Regardless of the element of the stem from which you lessen the vine, you have to though go away approximately 5 to 6 inches of stem related. Don't fear if there are more vines; they'll be trimmed away later.

The stem is crucial because it acts as a seal and forestalls the pumpkin from quick deteriorating. Avoid disposing of the pumpkin's stem by means of the use of the usage of pulling it. Carrying the pumpkin with the useful useful resource of its stem is risky, so in no manner do it.

How to Store Pumpkins

Leave at least an inch of the stem intact whilst harvesting pumpkins earlier than the number one frost.

The storage length is amongst 5 and 6 months.

Potatoes

Regardless of procedures you propose to use potatoes, all garden potatoes are harvested past due in the developing season. New potatoes, for you to be consumed proper away, are harvested before potatoes are meant for wintry climate storage.

When and How to Harvest Potatoes

Flowers and foliage determine the most dependable time to reap your crop. New potatoes ought to be harvested 2 to 3 weeks once they prevent flowering, and mature ones want to be harvested 2 to 3 weeks after the plant's foliage has withered.

If you preference to reap huge, ripe potatoes for garage, allow the plant to keep growing after it blooms.

Continue to mound the soil or comply with mulch throughout the plants to prevent the tubers from being uncovered to daylight.

Once the leaves at the pinnacle have withered, dig up your tubers with a garden fork.

The exceptional months to achieve potatoes are generally August or September, relying on the variety and developing environment.

How to Store Potatoes

After the flora have withered, potatoes want to be dug up and cured for 10 to fourteen days at 45 to 60 °F in a dark location.

Potatoes need to be saved among 40 and 45 °F when they were cured, as temperatures beneath forty°F may moreover additionally purpose them to end up overly sweet, whilst temperatures above 45 ° F can also additionally purpose sprouting.

Avoid storing near plant life that emit ethylene.

The garage duration is amongst four and 6 months.

Sweet Potatoes

Sweet potatoes are delicious and nutrient-dense, containing severa vitamins.

When and How to Harvest Sweet Potatoes

The skinny pores and pores and skin of newly dug potatoes makes them susceptible to sunburn. This have to allow pathogens to go into the tubers and harm them while they're being saved. If you want to reap sweet potatoes on a heat day, quick skip the roots to a shady location or cover them with a tarp.

The growing season largely determines at the same time as sweet potatoes are harvested. If the developing season has been favorable, with sufficient water and daylight, sweet potatoes can be harvested among 100 and a hundred and ten days after planting, depending on the variety.

As a fashionable rule, keep an eye fixed constant out for the earliest signs and symptoms and signs of leaf yellowing. This commonly occurs in late September or early October in advance than the first frost.

The timing and technique of candy potato harvesting are each vital.

The skin of candy potatoes is fragile and susceptible to tearing or bruising without issues, so make certain that your lawn fork is a long way enough from the plant's roots simply so they're not damaged.

How to Store Sweet Potatoes

Once the vines wither in late autumn, unearth the candy potatoes and pick the undamaged tubers for curing and storage.

Allow it to remedy for 5 to 10 days in a warmness (80 to eighty five°F) and humid (round 90%) environment. After curing, preserve them in a groovy, dry vicinity (fifty five to 60 ° F).

After in my opinion wrapping potatoes in paper, they'll be saved in ventilated packing containers or baskets.

The length of garage stages amongst 4 and 6 months.

Tomatoes

If you need to keep tomatoes at room temperature for extra than per week or so, you want first of all the proper range. Consider the Long Keeper Winter Storage tomato variety, that is designed for prolonged-term storage. These sorts are greater long lasting and may face up to prolonged storage.

Place unwashed, dry tomatoes in a garage field. How you pick to preserve the tomatoes is as much as you. Putting them in a container or basket with sheets of paper in among every layer is the fastest and easiest method. Tomatoes additionally can be saved in a canning jar's packaging subject, which must have separate cubicles for each tomato.

Tomatoes can be stored for up to 6 months in a groovy, darkish place. Put them within the basement or cellar to preserve them cool. Alternately, area them within the bottom of a closet or a few other vicinity that is hardly ever used.

Examine your tomatoes at least as quickly as each week for signs and signs and symptoms of mildew and decay. If one in all your tomatoes starts offevolved to rot, you may lose the entire amount. Rotate them every once in a while. They will ripen greater rapidly in areas in which they are in touch with the arena or basket.

Harvesting, making ready, and storing quit cease result and vegetables may additionally furthermore seem tough, however understanding the incredible manner to carry out your dreams makes the approach exciting.

Chapter 7: Creating Your Own Root Cellar

While canning and dehydrating are commonplace strategies for long term garage in the pantry, there are other long term storage alternatives as a manner to assist keep the freshness and taste of meat, end end result and greens.

Sure you may take a bushel of apples, peel them and device them into apple pie filling and it'll maintain within the freezer or a sealed jar for a long term. However there are nevertheless times when you need to chew down right into a glowing crisp apple. You want the crunch, the odor of real apple and the mild glaze of juice that clings for your chin.

For centuries humans saved things like apples, turnips, carrots and wintry weather squash with out using canning, dehydrating or traditional freezer luggage. Their solution modified into to show to properly concept out root cellars and distinct sorts of underground garage.

Now I recognize that to the informal layman a root cellar probably doesn't seem like plenty greater than a niche within the basement in that you keep meals subsequent to 3 antique boots and a pair tote packing containers of your teenager's antique toys.

However, the fact is that there is a lot of realistic garage technological understanding at art work. The variations in temperature, humidity and air drift paintings in live performance to sluggish the metabolic manner of ripening and rot for a extensive shape of vegetables.

Ideally, in case you're constructing your very very very own residence on your private home then it's clever to devise a place on the lowest degree that you can grow to be a root cellar. If you're in a situation like me, in which I sold a domestic that already had finished stages then you definitely definately definately may additionally want to improvise. I were given fortunate and the gasoline oil tank room changed into big sufficient, properly insulated and modestly ventilated enough that I modified into capable of convert it right into a make shift root cellar.

I actually have a friend that presently sold his very very own 20 acre spread and is inside the making plans section for the manner he desires to increase the living house. The home that already sits at the assets is one degree and no longer using a basement. Of route, long term garage is a primary factor for him.

He has household that when saved topics in an above ground root cellar carved into the factor of the hill. After some cautious research he wants to adapt that vintage idea into a modern standalone root cellar crafted from a carefully designed

outbuilding that could then be surrounded via a mound of earth.

This is called a mound root cellar. Pioneers at the Great Plains built them for decades from mounds of earth or rolls of sod constructed spherical crude timber structures.

My great grandmother had a root cellar like this inside the direction of the years at the same time as she and my remarkable grandfather had been residing in South Dakota. At the time, my outstanding grandfather changed into working for the railroad laying new tracks and upgrading vintage rail beds. This supposed that he had get entry to to vintage treated railroad timber. He used those to assemble a strong strengthened building. He crammed the cracks with dried grass then sealed the cracks with mortar. This essentially made a high-quality sturdy log cabin that he have become capable of mound with sandy floor.

For our purposes here, I think it makes for a extremely good opportunity to test the requirements that make an extraordinary root cellar work!

There are hundreds of factors to recall in making an powerful mound cellar, however, none of the opposite elements recall if the number one shape can't guide the burden of the soil mounded spherical and on top of it.

This may be quite a venture. I suggest you could't really run right proper right down to the sphere hardware hold and slap together a small shed which you shovel dirt over. You need something robust. Walls crafted from cinder block are reasonably-priced and easy to paintings with.

The ceiling is the real task. In principle my Great Grandfather's railroad timbers are a probable preference so long as you seal the cracks.

Personally I assume the quality concept is to borrow from a modern-day fashion I've seen popping up in campgrounds. More and further campgrounds are buying antique delivery boxes. They then burry them or mound them with soil to use as typhoon shelters or off season storage.

The mission is in locating a shipping container for the right rate that still may be introduced to you. It's not the shape of issue wherein you dial an 800 variety and a few man with sweat stains on his blouse hundreds it into the sector of his pickup truck and drops it off the next day.

As an exercise I did a few searching at the net and calling spherical. There have been severa businesses that had been inclined to sell me 20 and 40 foot long transport boxes. With shipping the final rate can also want to run in the $7,000-10,000 range!

There were many places that might rent me one but the proper away I described I might need to bury it in an above ground mound of soil, they refused to artwork with me.

It took approximately 10 hours of poking round earlier than I decided a delivery corporation with a trucking department that might promote me taken into consideration one in all their vintage 20 foot prolonged transport bins for $2,100.

To hold our exercising I were given a quote from a nearby building supply for a 20 foot via 20 foot via 10 foot immoderate brick constructing. Assuming that I can also do all the hard work myself, they came decrease back to me with a quote for $6, hundred.

Estimated production time for a do-it-yourselfer emerge as one hundred forty guy hours.

All subjects taken into consideration I would spend the extra time to really discover someone that modified into inclined to detail with an vintage shipping box so that you can consciousness at the web web site prep.

Site Prep

Once you've got got your imperative building or delivery container planned you'll need to pick out a website to location it. If you stay in a southern weather wherein summers are specially warm it might be extraordinary to orient the door on the north face. The door vicinity is the maximum possibly location wherein warmness from the out of doors international can leach in.

If you stay inside the northern location then the cold harsh winters are going to be your largest nemesis. I understand in which I live ambient low temperatures in the wintry weather can plunge down as low as -20. For the ones areas you want to orient the door managing south to capture any of the sun's strength.

I might also need to moreover do not forget constructing a buffer or a lobby location to restrict air change with the out of doors international whenever you open the door.

If you're going to be building a mound then drainage is part . Rain water desires someplace to move. So you need to ensure you have were given an adequate slope within the soil with an true sufficient amount of sand inside the soil. Clay soils can keep greater water including weight and growing the opportunities of corrosion. Planting grass may even assist with erosion.

General Root Cellar Principles

Whether you're building a mound style root cellar or converting a room on your unfinished basement there are a few stylish standards that you could need to plan for.

Temperature is one of the number one concerns for any root cellar. Adequate insulation can be very important at the same time as you consider that your exceptional aim temperature is forty levels. Of direction the temperature within the root cellar may be particular at the ceiling than it's miles at the floor. You can assume a 10 to 15 degree difference from top to bottom. The well-known window for optimum of the property you'll be placing up inside the root cellar is among 32 and 55 tiers.

Honestly the primary one year or you may probably want to examine this from an ordeal and blunders stand trouble. It's tough to truly recognize how lots insulation you'll want to put in. I needed to do a similar thing with the insulation in my barn to discover the proper stability amongst keeping the chickens heat and well ventilated.

What I did have grow to be turn to insulated panel board. I commenced out with 1 inch thick then I examined the temperature swing. When I determined out that I preferred greater insulation on the north and western walls I have emerge as I succesful of actually slide a 2 inch sheet into area. This end up a miles more versatile solution than in reality the use of roll out foam insulation.

You can use the temperature difference the various ground and the ceiling in your advantage. For example apples, potatoes and carrots will maintain better inside the temperatures close to the floor. Onions, garlic and shallots pick the warmer temperatures near the ceiling.

If you are into home brewing, a nicely-designed root cellar in truth holds the carboys at the perfect temperature for lager-fashion beer.

Humidity is the second one most critical element in a nicely-designed root cellar. With a touch cautious shopping you could discover a humidity gauge known as a hygrometer for round $20-25. Without modest to immoderate humidity most glowing stop result and vegetables will begin to shrivel. In well-known, a root cellar with a naked earth ground should have extra favorable humidity and require plenty less management than a root cellar with a poured concrete ground.

In my very very very own case, the room I changed in my already completed basement grow to be the room storing the gas oil tank and the properly pump. The gas oil simply acts like a warm temperature sink, whilst the pump and all the water lines

make contributions ambient humidity.

It simply happened to expose out that it worked exquisite for a root cellar. If you're not blessed with this many famous person-crossing factors you may want to expose to extremely good techniques of keeping humidity. In a few cases it's far as smooth as putting a shallow pan of warm water on the floor. The herbal warm temperature switch from the cold floor cooling down the water reasons humidity to upward thrust into the air. If you're in significantly dry conditions you'll likely have to reveal to exclusive alternatives like bringing a cold air humidifier in a few times regular with week.

If you are using your root cellar to hold dried gadgets then you may need to take greater precautions. Things like dried nuts and grains abhor excessive humidity. When I store rice and walnuts in my root cellar I choose to aspect them into 1 gallon zip pinnacle baggage. Then I seal the bags and keep them in totes. When I buy flour in bulk I need to preserve it in five gallon buckets with tight sealing lids.

Storing Notes

Apples pick out to be saved in temperatures among 33 and 40 stages and spherical ninety to ninety five% humidity. One of the maximum critical troubles to hold in thoughts with apples is that they slowly emit ethylene fuel through the years. This fuel motives improved ripening, spoilage and decay in masses of numerous vegetables. It's a large scenario for uncovered root vegetables stored close by. As such, potatoes, carrots and special root vegetables want to be stored as an extended manner far from apples as viable.

Apples want the bloodless to gradual down their ethylene production. Any bruised apples need to be removed from the batch. One bruise on a unmarried apple can certainly spoil the whole bunch thru a runaway ethylene cycle. An apple that is picked bloodless and allowed to warmth up then chilled down all over again will always not last as long as an apple this is stored cold from the primary minute it is picked from the tree.

Beets and Carrots select temperatures amongst 32 and 40 stages and 90 to ninety five% humidity. One massive gain is they can truely be stored in buckets full of unfastened, dried playground sand.

Pull them proper now from the ground and do no longer wash them. If in any respect possible you need to try and harvest them after 2 to 3 days of dry weather. Harvesting them subsequently of wet weather or washing them after picking invites

water into the small dents and divots which later can grow to be little festering pockets of rot.

Snip the tops to head away round 1 inch of the green uncovered from the nub. Fill the buckets half of of of manner with sand. Then stand the beets and carrots up and lace extra dry sand spherical them. Kept this way beets and carrots can preserve over for three to 4 months. You can set the buckets of sand on the ground of the foundation cellar below the cabinets wherein carrots will revel in the cool temps. In reality while you located nutrient wealthy, lawn grown root vegetables at temperatures simply above freezing the flavors begin to slowly accentuate!

Brussels Sprouts are unusual vegetables in that if you cautiously do away with them from the garden soil and pot them up, the plant will hold generating harvestable sprouts in your root cellar for multiple weeks. I'd suggest the use of a five gallon bucket with nitrogen rich, black loam soil. Pull them from your garden after they've been exposed to as a minimum one or 2 mild frosts. This will help concentrate the taste within the sprouts that increase in your cellar potting.

Cabbage may be a exquisite keeper for the foundation cellar in case you choose the proper emblem. Otherwise you are probable better off selecting to gadget and ferment the cabbage into sauerkraut. Red cabbage has a bent to preserve better in a root cellar than green. Some of the awesome sorts for the foundation cellar are Brunswick, Danish Ballhead, Late Flat Dutch and Red Acre. Harvest the heads the day after the primary frost. Pull the flowers right now from the ground, use a sharp knife to reduce off the bottom of the top from the thick root then take away the extra free leaves from the top. This want to depart you with a nub at the lowest that stands proud about an inch.

Over time cabbage can begin to supply off a sturdy odor that may pervade your root cellar. I genuinely opt to wrap the cabbage heads in newspaper then p.C. Them loosely proper into a sealable garage tote. I try to depart a few area in a few of the heads, retaining the heads form proper now touching through the usage of balls of crumpled newspaper.

Dried Beans are a nice thing to maintain round as long as they'll be very well dried and sealed away. Since beans are this kind of amazing manner to regenerate lawn soil, I constantly turn out to be with way too a whole lot of them. Dried beans are a high-quality addition to soups, particularly if you're making stock from extra bones on the save you of searching season.

Allow the pods to genuinely ripen at the vine. You need to listen the pods rattle with the free beans interior. Pick the pods from the flowers and vicinity them on a unmarried layer sheet pan covered with newspaper in a dark dry vicinity for 10 days to two weeks.

Shell a few beans as a take a look at. You want to make certain they will be dry enough that your fingernail received't dent them. If they may be very well dry, shell them and carefully dispose of any extra debris. I like to put them up in sealed glass jars to keep them cold but uninfluenced with the useful resource of the basis cellars immoderate humidity.

Garlic should be pulled simply due to the fact the tops are loss of existence. You want to drag them after 2 to a few days of dry climate. Brush off the loose soil together with your arms but do not wash them. Place them in a groovy, darkish, dry and properly ventilated location for 2 to three weeks to permit them to cure.

Once they're cured you can braid the withered tops together. I'm for my part quite awful at braiding some element inclusive of my daughter's hair, so I forgo the braiding, snip the tops andkeep them in some of my partner's vintage nylons.

G arlic doesn't just like the excessive humidity of the principle root cellar, so I want to cling it in part of my garage in any other case I will duct tape the nylons onto a bucket lid, then seal them in a five gallon bucket with a handful of painter's desiccant within the backside. Just ensure the nylon isn't placing so low within the bucket that it touches the desiccant.

Kept this manner they could ultimate five to 6 months.

Onions have a hint leeway relying upon how you decided to set up them. About 33% of the onions I plant each spring are mounted shallow to the point of shaping into fulling measured bulbs. A huge portion of my onion devices are planted further so they come up as scallions. This is an character inclination component because of the reality this kind of large amount my cooking and barbecuing uses scallions. Definitely I truly have a few scallions that don't get applied and they spend the pre-fall preventing in competition to the heaviness of the dust to emerge as hindered pearl onions.

Onions ought to be amassed after the tops have grow to be yellow and certainly surpassed directly to the exquisite beyond decrease returned. In a top notch international they have to be accumulate following 2 to three days of dry weather. Be that as it is able to, you could as an opportunity now not leave them inside the floor too lengthy after the tops have absolutely surpassed on all over again or they could smash. This is in particular obvious in wet soil. Assuming that you comprehend the repair is starting to kick the bucket once more essentially however isn't

definitely executed and you see a first-rate period of moist weather in the prolonged gauge, then, at that factor, I ought to drag them in advance of time desk to maintain them dry.

You can tidy a part of the soil off the onions with your thoughts, however don't wash them. A moist onion welcomes decay in a bigger range of approaches than one!

Once they will be pulled location the onions on sheet field fixed with paper in a fab, stupid, dry and all spherical ventilated spot for two to 3 weeks to allow them to repair. The restoration time for over mature scallions or pearl onions is more restrained. They clearly assume 10 to fourteen days.

Once they're relieved you could cut back any leftover tops. Simply try to leave an inch or two of head over the bulb to maintain it again from being uncovered. Very similar to garlic onions incline in the direction of dry conditions. Instead I need to maintain it in a part of my storage otherwise I will duct tape the nylons onto a bucket lid, then seal them in a five gallon bucket with a handful of painter's desiccant in the backside. Simply make sure the nylon isn't putting so low inside the pail that it contacts the desiccant.

Kept this way they'll remaining 6 to 7 months.

Parsnips are essentially much like carrots, aside from they have got little capacity to endure progressive ice activities. Collect parsnips following the number one ice of the autumn. Pull them straightforwardly from the start don't wash them. Then clip the greens an inch or above the premise. Fill five gallon cans most of the way with sand. Then stand the parsnips up and lace extra dry sand round them. Kept this way parsnips can maintain over for a chunk whilst. You can set the boxes of sand at the floor of the foundation basement close to the carrots and beets.

Pears are very similar to apples in that a swollen pear will emit an excessive degree of ethylene making the the rest of the package deal deal destroy. I for the most thing determine to can wounded pears. On the off chance that one is in reality someplace down inside the dog house I'll channel it to the chickens as a natural product snack.

Wrap every pear in paper with paper or cardboard spacers very much like you would heads of cabbage. Store them in cardboard cubicles, timber boxes or vintage milk boxes. When actually essential a stable garb bushel can get you with the useful resource of. They keep better spherical 32 stages, so it's extremely good to set them at the ground. With a tad of karma and cool temps you want to have the selection to get 6 to approximately months out of them. Assuming you hearth starting them up and they're searching brown inside it's an instance that everything goes to move awful. I would possibly can the top notch ones and remodel any horrible ones into manure or chook snacks.

Potatoes want to be reaped after the highest factor of the flora have absolutely gave up the ghost once more. Attempt to allow three or 4 days of dry weather to skip previous to accumulating them. Potatoes which can be collected moist or washed actually after acquire will extra regularly than not decay swiftly from the miniscule measures of water that in truth wait in the eyes.

Potatoes have to be relieved earlier than they'll be positioned into extended haul stockpiling. Leave them messy and in a silly dry spot round 50 to 60 tiers for 10 to fourteen days. This will permit the skins to thicken and allow a part of the regular sugars to change into lengthy haul, stockpiling amicable starch.

Once they have got relieved, you should then save them at temps round 40 to 45 ranges. Assuming that the ground of your root basement is close to freezing you may want to strive not to keep them there. Temps near freezing could make the dampness freeze inside the potato even as passing at the sugars to assume. This gives you a potato with a brand new candy flavor.

Squash and Pumpkins are profoundly nutritious and are exceedingly famous choices for extended haul stockpiling. Reap all squash and pumpkins earlier than the precept ice or at the same time as the plant interfacing the plant to the natural product bites the dirt. Here and there sugar pumpkins can mature as quick as August. Assuming this takes place select out fast or they may rot.

Make certain at the same time as you pick out the flora that you leave the stem in truth appended. Assuming you pull the stem off the herbal product it's going to make a spot that welcomes decay. I've located inside the past that squash and pumpkins which have been authorized to take a seat on the soil in area of straw are positive to foster shape at the pores and skin over the long haul. To counter this I like to offer the outer layer of every natural product a speedy wipe down with a mixture of dye and water. It doesn't take a ton of fade, four tablespoons in a solitary gallon of cold water is more than enough.

I wipe them down to kill any anticipated spores from their experience at the dirt. Then, at that element, I towel them dry with easy paper towels.

Most squash and pumpkins want to answer for a quick period in warm temperature temps round eighty tiers. Typically seven days in a heat, dry, stupid spot will suffice.

Acorn squash needn't trouble with this restoring time, however they moreover don't maintain so long as precise assortments like butternut.

Once they may be relieved you may located them on a middle rack in your root basement. I want to hold the herbal products decrease back from contacting via using setting cardboard spacers or little wads of paper in the center of every one.

Early on this doesn't depend huge variety in any respect however as I'm stretch ing my stash of butternut squash out into the month of March I locate that those which may be touching in competition to every extraordinary without delay start to increase a shape of bruised spot.

When doubtful of thumb pumpkins can remaining 6 probable 7 months. Sugar pumpkins which might be saved cool can ultimate five to a half of of 12 months as can butternut squash.

Sweet Potatoes need to be dove up from the nursery within the fall, ideally following 2 to three days of warmth climate. Just dismiss the soil of them alongside side your hands. Washing them welcomes decay to create inside the wrinkles, imprints and eyes. They favored to be relieved in warmness temperatures spherical eighty to eighty 5 and excessive mugginess. It's with the useful aid of and large the shape of situations you may be searching beforehand to assuming you observe a pleasant stretch of "Indian Summer" at the drawn out forecast.

Allow them to restoration on a sheet dish steady with paper in a warmth, all spherical ventilated spot for 7 to 10 days previous to transferring them into lengthy haul stockpiling. The perfect temperature for extended haul stockpiling is round 55 to 60 stages, however they'll certainly do first-rate and dandy across the mid 40's to low 50's.

Wrap them gently in paper and preserve them in a ventilated spot in a wooden field or vintage milk carton.

Stored because it ought to be you may preserve them for four or five months. In the occasion that a couple of begin to deliver symptoms of turning bitter I could probably haul them out of the bunch, reduce out the horrible spots and located them in the fertilizer or feed them as a treat to the chickens.

This is typically your admonition sign that you have a ton of yam pie in your destiny!

Turnips are essentially similar to carrots, aside from they've got little capability to undergo modern ice events and lean closer to marginally clammy conditions in their sand packing containers. Collect turnips following the principle ice of the fall. Pull them straightforwardly from the beginning don't wash them. Basically reduce the veggies an inch or over the foundation. Fill five gallon cans maximum of the manner with sand. Then combo some moist sphagnum moss in equal parts with playground sand. Stand the turnips up and bind the sand and damp sphagnum greenery round them. Kept this way turnips can hold over for 12 to 14 weeks. You can set the cans of sand on the ground of the basis basement near the carrots and beets.

Chapter 8: Canning

Obviously canning isn't simply as regards to loading up dietary nutritional dietary supplements and calories in a field to keep over for added slim sports later inside the year. There are certainly one of a type exciting factors in ground, flavor and shading. To make certain you're saving each one of the additives of the goods of the soil you're canning you want to preserve constant at the strategies from the preliminary step to the remaining.

Properly canned meals is nutritious, tasty, pleasurable to the eye or more all else protected to eat.

On paper canning is a fairly clean interplay in that you region the food being stated in a sanitized glass subject. You warmness the sphere in a water shower, which disinfects any microorganisms or organisms in the food, even as likewise solving the pinnacle on the jar.

For the giant majority the water bathe is pretty a good deal as

honest as a huge canning pot wherein the packing containers are reduced in water that covers the top of the field by using someplace round inches. Certain human beings need to make this a stride further and make use of a anxiety cooker.

Advocates of the strain cooker approach like to disinfect under tension due to the fact the pressure vessel allows you to attain at temperatures over 212 degrees. 212 is the first-class temperature that you could heat water to earlier than it goes to steam. In the tension vessel you can on occasion arrive at temperatures however immoderate as 240 stages!

The reality may be that a big part of the things you 're apprehensive approximately bite the dust once they hit the 160 five to 100 seventy diploma range. Obviously, a definitive horrible beastie organism that torment the canning universe is Botulism. Botulism, on the same time as dealt with without delay on the health facility is a hopeless enduring stumble upon. Without set off remedy it can disable and kill you in horrible techniques.

Advocates of the stress canner technique will allow you to recognize that it's the awesome way to kill botulism spores in canned meals types. On paper that is accurate and if you have any worries approximately botulism spores or pollutants developing in any of your canned goods, you then have to show to the stress cooker method.

The botulism spore bites the dust in a flash at 240 tiers. At lesser temperatures it takes extra time to kill it. The basic precept to consider while making use of an unpressurized water bathe is which you need to keep the meals in the discipline at 100 eighty

degrees for 10 mins to viably kill botulism.

Again this seems to be straightforward. Bubbling for 10 mins at 100 80 doesn't look like this type of problem from the get flow.

The problem is that it's the meals temperature we're discussing. So at the off threat that it's miles going into the field at room temperature and is then positioned into effervescent water, it dreams a virtually best possibility to warmth as much as one hundred 80 previous being held there for 10 mins. Then it wants to quiet down yet again.

For exceptional merchandise of the soil being warmed for this lengthy should cause them to turn tender. Salted pepperoncini peppers as an example will remodel into withered mush as an alternative efficaciously following 10 minutes at a hundred 80 and a gradual loosen up.

It is critical to pay attention to that botulism is mainly awful for babies under a 12 months antique as their lacking belly related frameworks arise brief on the acidic concord to sufficient battle the spores and poisons. If you are an advocate of the best hundred eighty for 10 mins technique, then I strongly advise you alter your final cooking method in advance than supporting a toddler that is under three hundred and sixty five days of age.

Anything that isn't canned via the use of using the use of the strain approach should again be cooked to some element like one hundred and 80 stages for 10 minutes before serving.

There are techniques you can use to take a seat lower back the containers off faster than basically forgetting approximately them at the counter, however they may be created with their personal dangers. Throwing a warmness box in an ice water bathe is certain to stun and destroy the glass of the box than it's miles to sit back the meals down.

Water Bath Canning

Personally I surely love the water shower method, despite all of its capability botulism pit falls. A couple of years lower once more my strain canner dropped a big load on me. I were given a frightful steam eat on my arm and I emerge as a bit in need of coins so I went to the a hundred and eighty for 10 minutes method. For maximum food kinds this works, however there are more than one specific instances and provisos which I'll be aware as we cross along.

As a vast rule, meals sorts with immoderate corrosiveness are a lot much less willing to foster tainting from risky organisms. The ordinary acids make an adverse climate for them to create in. There are some food sources in which this may be especially thrilling. A few forms of tomatoes have plenty much less corrosive and require the growth of a touch lemon juice to punch up their pH for canning.

Equipment you can need for the water bathtub approach

An big inventory pot or canning pot with a lid

Mason jars

Clean, rust unfastened rings

New tops with new smooth corporations A brace for taking care of bins Welding glove (Optional) Cooling rack

Basic Procedure

This can trade a touch from one components to a few one of a kind, so view at this as a favored guiding precept.

Step 1: Inspect all packing containers, jewelry and tops. Dispose of any boxes that have chips or breaks at the lip. Try no longer to make use of earrings with rust inside and, usually widespread of all, continuously make use of each different top. When a top has been warmed it is able to't be reused.

Attempting to do as such makes a helpless seal that can permit microorganisms in.

Step 2: Fill the pot with an unobtrusive measure of excessive temp water. Attempt to check the water dislodging for the amount of containers you'll location inside the water bathe. It is in the end higher to have lots of water within the pot than sufficiently no longer. You can employ a Pyrex estimating cup or soup spoon to do away with abundance water.

Step three: Place the pot on the oven on immoderate warmth.

Step four: Once the water begins offevolved to stew, deliver down the unfilled packing containers and rings into the water. Try no longer to feature the covers. Permit them to bubble for 10 minutes. Then dispose of them with a sturdy tongs or the jar clamp. Pour away any overabundance water and set them at the cooling rack to calm down.

Step five: Prepare the goods of the soil as in step with the precise recipe. Step 6: Pour or spoon the meals into the containers. Give each region a bit tap or shake to free any stuck air bubbles. Step 7: Use a spotless tea towel or paper towel to wipe the lip of every jar.

This is large to get a respectable seal.

Step 8: Carefully region the cover on top of the box. Be positive no longer to permit your arms to the touch in the elastic ring.

Step 9: Place the jewelry up and over and connect them down. I discover it's less difficult

to keep the field with a welding glove.

Step 10: Allow the containers to sit down for 5 mins to alleviate the temperature contrasts amongst all of the certainly one of a type factors.

Step 11: Place the bins carefully into the large pot of effervescent water. Ensure the very excellent point of the field is included by means of manner of the use of some component like 2 creeps of water. Permit them to bubble for the time confirmed within the technique. Remember that on the equal time as trying a few different device the bottom put together meal time in each case want to be 10 minutes or more.

Step 12: Remove the containers from the pot of bubbling water making use of the field clip. I for one have a welding glove that I decided out the manner to healthful a large elastic glove over pinnacle of which allows me to straightforwardly deal with the jars.

Step 13: Allow the bins to take a seat down undisturbed for six hours, but a whole day is probably perfect. On the off chance that you address the bins too early when they emerge from the water bathe the sensitive seal can be damaged.

Step 14: Use an indelible marker to name the top of the sector with the additives call and the date.

Pressure Cooker Canning

This technique is the favored method for saving low corrosive substance food types simply as meats, much like hamburger, venison, chicken and special varieties of fish. I need to concede that my remaining anxiety cooker became a modest version that regular ineffectively and had a expertise for the seal staying. It is nicely worth the try and spend the extra cash to get a incredible tension cooker implied for canning massive batches.

Equipment you could want for the stress cooker method Pot-type autoclave or massive stress

cooker Mason jars

Clean, rust loose earrings

New covers with new clean

organizations A clasp for taking

care of bins Welding

glove (Optional) Cooling

rack

Kitchen timer

Basic Procedure

This can differ a hint from one components to each other, so view at this as a critical rule. Ensure you look at the manufacturer's bearings truely previous to making use of the pressure cooker.

High corrosive meals resources require much less pounds of tension within the vessel than low corrosive food types. Overall immoderate corrosive food types require a base 6 kilos of hysteria for every square inch.

Low corrosive meals belongings require a benchmark of eleven PSI.

It is essential to be privy to that the time and strain preferred for every components will range relying for your peak. When unsure of thumb you must gather 1 pound of tension for every 2,000 toes you are above ocean degree.

For example in the event that you inhabit 6,000 toes above ocean degree and you had been canning a low corrosive food you may need to work at thirteen PSI.

Step 1: Inspect all containers, jewelry and covers. Dispose of any boxes which have chips or breaks on the lip. Try no longer to make use of rings with rust inner and typically huge of all normally employ some distinctive cover. When a top has been warmed it is able to't be reused.

Attempting to do as such makes a helpless seal which can permit microorganisms in.

Step 2: Place the framework that determined the pressure cooker inside the lower a part of the pot and cargo up with water as tons because the maker's predetermined degree. A few devices have a line carved within the metal on the same time as others essentially employ an expressed amount.

Step three: Prepare the method as noted.

Step 4: Pour the food into the packing containers and wipe the lip of the glass field easy. Stage five: Use a spotless tea towel or paper towel to

wipe the lip of each jar.

This is full-size to get a decent seal.

Step 6: Carefully area the duvet on pinnacle of the container. Be sure no longer to allow your hands to the touch in the elastic ring.

Step 7: Place the jewelry up and over and connect them down. I count on that it's far' less tough to preserve the sector with a welding glove.

Step 8: Allow the bins to sit down for five minutes to mild the temperature contrasts between all the one-of-a-kind elements.

Step 9: Tighten the jewellery onto the jars.

Step 10: Place the boxes in the water. Twofold test that the volume is within the maker's expressed solid levels.

Step 11: Put the duvet on with out the pipe cap. Turn the hotness of the oven as lots as immoderate and permit the water to bubble for five minutes with the steam coming out.

Step 12: Place the pressure cap at the vessel. Then, at that thing, display the time and tension in step with the recipe.

Step 13: When it arrives on the predefined measure of time, transfer the hotness off and allow the pot to chill till the pressure check peruses zero.

Step 14: Remove the containers from the pot of effervescent water the use of the box brace. I for one have a welding glove that I discovered out the manner to healthful a huge elastic glove over pinnacle of which lets in me to straightforwardly cope with the jars.

Step 15: Allow the boxes to sit down undisturbed for six hours, however a whole day may be perfect. Assuming you control the bins too early once they emerge from the water shower the touchy seal may be damaged.

Step sixteen: Use an indelible marker to name the cover of the sphere with the method name and the date.

NOTE: Whether you are the use of the anxiety cooker technique or the water bathe approach all tops must be packed descending every time they may be cooled. Any covers that pop while you faucet them are not as predicted regular and is probably unsafe to installation in storage.

If this takes place you want to rehash the interplay creating a issue to honestly wipe the lips of the glass and continuously utilize a brand new lid.

Canning Procedures which can be NOT Recommended

There are one-of-a-kind strategies which have emerged over the course of the years for individuals who attempted to be innovative with the disinfection method.

Oven canning is a method in that you location the uncooked meals assets into packing containers and placed the bins in a warmness broiler. You basically put together the boxes for a while till the little elastic seals at the covers liquefy and companion with the glass of the jar.

The authentic hassle with this approach is the helpless hotness bypass. Air conducts heat more than one times extra sluggish than water. Indeed, assuming that you put an ice robust shape in a gallon of tepid water and put an indistinguishable ice three-D rectangular in a 3 hundred diploma range the ice block within the tepid water will liquefy masses faster!

What takes vicinity with a canning subject to your variety is that the fieriness of the air liquefies the hoop a while earlier than any of that hotness figures out the way to flow into through the included glass and into the meals. Since you haven't any real manner to check the temperature of the meals inside the field you can basically be fixing in an entire host of evil pathogens.

I had a partner whose mom modified right into a strong supporter of this technique. She didn't really be for the cause that me and all my communicate about helpless hotness circulate. So we directed a check and installation a container of all spherical everyday nursery tomatoes in the broiler technique.

Once she became persuaded that the duvet had gotten itself on we hauled the sector out of the variety, flew off the top and glued a 2nd look at test thermometer into the focus of the tomatoes. It have a look at a disturbing a hundred and ten degrees! Fundamentally now not absolutely had it unnoticed to kill any ability botulism spores it without delay up hadn't killed any possibly microbes. Sometimes she had mounted the satisfactory climate for unsafe microorganisms to elevate. Her garage room have become hypothetically a weapon of mass obliteration destined for the district sincere!

The following day her fertilizer heap were given masses bigger and her monetary balance had been given a hint greater modest whilst she bought a stress canner!

Pre-cooking or untreated canning is every other likely perilous approach. The idea in the again of it's miles which you prepare dinner the meals earlier then area it straight away in jars and seal them. The expectation is that the hotness of the prepared food might be to the factor of liquefying and starting off the seals.

On paper this approach isn't absolutely terrible, but it's miles none the a great deal less stacked with promising conditions for organisms to get in. Any botulism spores that can be inside the field or on the top acquired't have been warmed to the issue of killing them. Truth be recommended there's the genuine capability for special microorganisms to get through the usage of inside the constrained quantity of air location a number of the maximum problem of the food and the decrease a part of the lid.

Also the duvet might not 100 percent seal. There is a real opportunity that the encircling hotness of the meals set in the discipline will leave a segment of ring unaffected. This makes a hint air hollow wherein organisms can get into the field over the long haul and begin breeding.

Microwave canning is one greater innovative however unstable approach for fixing and defend canned merchandise. Indeed, even the first-rate microwave is stunningly conflicting in how the producer warms the inner area. I tried it as quickly as slightly out of interest

and what I wound up with emerge as a container of strawberries wherein some berries had been rocket warm and others had been really lukewarm. There changed into furthermore a unusual engineered odor that I can also have as an alternative not play with.

www.ingramcontent.com/pod-product-compliance
Lightning Source LLC
Chambersburg PA
CBHW070557010526
44118CB00012B/1348